THE SUCCESS
OF RUSSIAN
ECONOMIC
REFORMS

The Royal Institute of International Affairs is an independent body which promotes the rigorous study of international questions and does not express opinions of its own. The opinions expressed in this publication are the responsibility of the author.

THE SUCCESS
OF RUSSIAN
ECONOMIC
REFORMS

Brigitte Granville

THE ROYAL INSTITUTE OF
INTERNATIONAL AFFAIRS
International Economics Programme

© Royal Institute of International Affairs, 1995

Published in Great Britain in 1995 by the Royal Institute of International Affairs,
Chatham House, 10 St James's Square, London SW1Y 4LE
(Charity Registration No. 208 223).

Distributed worldwide by The Brookings Institution, 1775 Massachusetts Avenue, NW,
Washington, DC 20036-2188, USA.

British Library Cataloguing in Publication Data
A CIP catalogue record for this book is available from the British Library.

ISBN 1 899658 06 8

Text set in Bembo.
Printed and bound in Great Britain by Redwood Books.

To Christopher

CONTENTS

ABOUT THE AUTHOR

Brigitte Granville is a Senior Research Fellow in the International Economics Programme at the Royal Institute of International Affairs. She is a former member of the Macroeconomic and Financial Unit of the Ministry of Finance of the Russian Federation and consultant of the European Expertise Service (EES).

PREFACE AND ACKNOWLEDGMENTS

This is a tightly focused study. It makes no attempt to be magisterial; indeed the attempt would be vain with so little time available for a larger perspective, and so little supporting documentation.

In this study I concentrate on the macroeconomic events of this turbulent period. I note, of course, the key political decisions which had an important macroeconomic impact, but I have firmly resisted all requests to write more about the political dynamics of the new Russian state. I understand these requests: I have been privileged to have a remarkable close-up view throughout this extraordinary historical episode. Nonetheless, I am not a political scientist, and I believe the politics of Russia deserves truly expert attention.

There is, of course, far more to reform than macroeconomics: privatization, the construction of new institutions and the assurance of property rights, the adjustment of popular attitudes, an appropriate and acceptable social policy, for example. The macroeconomics have, however, been central to the successful establishment of a market economy in Russia, and I concentrate mainly on the monetary aspect.

This book has two sources. The intellectual foundation is the training in monetary economics I received from Emil Maria Claassen. The book's substance is the product of my work in Russia since 1991, which has been largely the fruit of opportunities given me by Anders Åslund and Jeffrey Sachs. I have been fortunate to have as colleagues in Moscow Peter Boone, Jacques Delpla, Torun Hedback and Judith Shapiro. I should also like to thank Barry Ickes and Vincent Koen. All my other colleagues at the Macroeconomic and Financial Unit (MFU) of the Finance Ministry of the Russian Federation are gratefully acknowledged.

The last part of my work has been made possible by my position, arranged by Neil Parisson, as expert to the European Expertise Service, where I am particularly grateful to Peter Oppenheimer for reading and commenting so carefully on the first draft of this book. I am also extremely grateful to Ellie Bucharskaya for her excellent assistance.

Among my Russian colleagues and friends, I would especially like to thank Mstislav Afanasiev, Ludmila Goldina, Patricia Isayeva, Andrei Illarionov, Vladimir Kosmarsky, Andrei Lushin, Vladimir Mau, Alexander Naumenkov, Sergei Pavlenko, Vladimir Smenkovski, Sergei Vasilyev and Mrs Tchumachenko.

In the Royal Institute of International Affairs, I would like to thank Mary Bone, Vincent Cable, Hannah Doe, Susan Franck, Margaret May and Fionnuala O'Flynn.

My work in Moscow has been financed first by the Ford Foundation and then by the European Union inside the TACIS programme, as well as the TACIS-ACE 1991 programme. All are gratefully acknowledged; but responsibility for the content of this book of course remains entirely my own.

July 1995   Brigitte Granville

'*The economic system of Russia has undergone and is undergoing such rapid changes that it is impossible to obtain a precise and accurate account of it ... Almost everything one can say about the country is true and false at the same time.*'

KEYNES *A SHORT VIEW ON RUSSIA* (1925)
QUOTED IN KOEN AND MEYERMANS (1994)

INTRODUCTION

The first quarter of 1995 was the most decisive and radical period in Russian economic reform since price liberalization at the beginning of 1992. Throughout this period, the main macroeconomic problem faced by the Russian government was high inflation, defined as 'averaging more than 15% per month (435% per year) for several months' (Dornbusch, 1990b, p. 6). After hope of stabilization in the spring of 1994, economic reform in Russia had been thrown back to the verge of collapse. Three full years after the beginning of reforms in January 1992, the monthly inflation rate in January 1995 rose to 17.8%, while on 6 January, with the Central Bank's reserves all but exhausted, the authorities narrowly averted a rouble crisis which in its scale and consequences would have dwarfed the 'Black Tuesday' of October 1994. The crisis of those days was brought to a head by the war in Chechenia, then at its height.

Yet the government not only preserved the existing achievements of economic reform but also, in the face of severe adversity, forged the keys to a successful and hitherto elusive macroeconomic stabilization. The critical measures were in two areas: first, foreign trade liberalization, especially in the oil sector, which both removed the basis for some of the worst official corruption, and increased revenue; and, secondly, the adoption of a budget without monetary financing of the deficit and, in related measures, the halting of centralized credits from the Central Bank and arbitrary off-budget expenditure (presidential decree no. 244, February 1995). All these steps made possible an agreement with the IMF on a 'standby' credit of SDR 435 billion.

Russian reforms are often perceived in the West as if the reforms themselves are the cause of severe economic instability, with market-oriented policies faltering against a background of falling living standards and overall economic deterioration. This view assumes that programmes aiming at macroeconomic stabilization through a tight monetary and fiscal policy have failed to revive growth. In this book the opposite thesis is defended: that the road to stabilization was lengthened by a tendency to half-measures (anything but 'shock therapy'), and that the persistent high inflation that resulted was the fundamental obstacle to an investment-based recovery.

At the beginning of 1992 the Russian government intended to implement a comprehensive stabilization programme, under the impression that foreign aid would come in the middle of that year to help make this programme sustainable. However, the key elements in this projected aid programme (such as a $6 billion stabilization fund) never materialized. Instead, a situation arose reminiscent of Brezhnevite stagnation, whereby the West would pretend to aid the Russians while they would pretend to stabilize.[1] But still the process of economic reforms went on; and in the intervening period the Russian economy has been transformed.

Russia has had to deal with a highly negative inheritance, but every year since the beginning of economic reform parts of the Soviet legacy were superseded:

- 1992 was the year of price liberalization: it was also the year when industrial lobbies successfully used inter-enterprise arrears as a lever to obtain cheap financing. As a result huge subsidized credits were allocated to state firms, at a damaging cost to the economy as a whole. But the lesson was learned, and, despite regular attempts by enterprise directors to intimidate the authorities with the spectre of a new arrears crisis, the government gradually moved from Central Bank bail-outs to market-based solutions, assisted by a new federal commission on insolvent (bankrupt) enterprises.
- 1993 saw the end of the rouble zone, which in 1992 had cost Russia between 6% and 10% of GDP (see Granville, 1994; Granville and Lushin, 1993).
- 1993 also saw the end of the 1977 Soviet constitution. One immediate result of this fundamental political change was that the Central Bank for the first time aligned itself seriously with the anti-inflation stance of the government. By mid-1994 fiscal and monetary tightening, together with successful completion of the voucher privatization process, had attracted the first major wave of foreign portfolio investments into Russia. However, once again the process of stabilization fell victim to hostile forces: not only 'seasonal factors' such as the perennial credits to

agriculture, but also the conjunction of an old phenomenon (a loose monetary policy) with a new one (the emergence of financial markets).

The stabilization breakthrough of 1995 was therefore founded on a process of incremental gains which, though positive in itself, does not represent the sum of Russian achievement in the sphere of economic reform. Equally important was the suppression of a political–economic vicious circle which during the first two years of transition (1992–3) undermined prospects of any real macrostabilization. The heart of this problem lay in so-called 'directed credits', which were funds provided directly by the Central Bank to favoured enterprises exposed for the first time to market costs and falling market demand (in place of reduced state orders) for their products. This credit system, which was the principal cause of high inflation, was sustained by the political conditions obtaining in Russia in 1992–3.

During the first half of 1992, the reformers around Prime Minister Yegor Gaidar made their plans on the assumption that a tough fiscal and monetary stance would achieve both macrostabilization and microeconomic restructuring as a result of the financial discipline and incentives for enterprises created by the collapse of demand and by the opening of the economy. Unfortunately, Central Bank credits to state enterprises were relaxed in the second half of 1992 as a result of pressure applied by state enterprises. Even now government transfers to state enterprises remain a threat, although a substantially reduced one, to the stability of the Russian economy. The first massive injection of new credits in 1992 came as the effects of the market conditions introduced by Gaidar's government began to bite in many parts of Russian industry, especially in the defence-related enterprises where state orders had been slashed. Funds were allocated to specific enterprises in a manner that reflected the bargaining and political power of the recipients rather than on the basis of market considerations, and irrespective of the fact that no single injection of new credits could solve the problem of inter-enterprise arrears. These arrears helped loss-making enterprises to transform a problem of particular firms into a general problem and to undermine the stabilization policy by getting refinancing without having to restructure. Inflation was driven by the belief (which proved to be right) that arrears were money (World Bank, 1992, p. 20).

Such lax monetary policy was made possible not so much by the nature of the pressures common to a certain extent to all economies in transition, but by the conflict that developed from mid-1992 to October 1993 between the government and the Central Bank. This reflected the fundamental divide between the government, composed of reformers, and the parliament, composed mainly of old Soviet placemen or fairweather democrats who turned sour when not appointed to positions in the new government. Indeed, the legacy of the Soviet parliamentary system considerably weakened the reform process and handed an extremely powerful instrument to its opponents. As Yeltsin remarked in his memoirs, 'without political backup, Gaidar's reforms were left hanging in midair. Indeed, this was an era of issues hanging in midair. Laws not passed in final draft, incoherent decisions taken. It was the era that finally brought the country to October 1993' (Yeltsin, 1994, p. 127). The Central Bank (CBR) was subordinate to the Supreme Soviet and independent of the government and the President (Popov, 1994).[2] While in Western countries central bank independence from government is associated with monetary rectitude, in Russia that same independence, or rather responsibility to the anti-reform parliament, was the first main cause of lax monetary policy. The second cause was Viktor Gerashchenko, the former head of the Soviet Gosbank, who was appointed chairman of the CBR in July 1992, confirmed in post by parliament in November 1992 and only finally removed on 14 October 1994. One of the reasons why Gaidar agreed to what turned out to be such a damaging appointment was Gerashchenko's stature as a 'professional' banker capable of sorting out the administrative chaos into which the CBR had fallen.[3] In the West, he was respected for having always serviced Soviet debt. Gerashchenko's avowed preference for a lax monetary stance, and his strong belief that his responsibilities included the formation and implementation of industrial policy, won influential political support from a centrist grouping led by large state enterprise managers, notably from the defence sector. The most influential in this period (1992–3) was Arkady Volsky, head of the Union of Industrialists and Entrepreneurs, described by Yeltsin (1994, p. 168) as 'essentially a lobbying organisation for large government-subsidised industries'. This Union was itself part of the Civic Alliance political grouping, 'a centrist group favouring gradual reform to protect the large industries' (Yeltsin, 1994, p. 168), which was instrumental in bringing about the removal of Gaidar from the premiership at the Congress of People's Deputies in December 1992. Its members argued that the approach favoured by Gaidar would destroy the country's industrial base.

The conflict between the reformers and the parliament continued throughout the period 1992–4. It was basically a conflict between those who believed that inflation was a monetary phenomenon (namely the reformers, led by Gaidar and the Finance Minister) and those (prominent among them Geraschenko) who believed that inflation was the result of supply-side factors such as monopolistic pricing and deregulation of energy prices (Popov, 1994, p. 10). With the money supply increasing on average by 20% a month, Gerashchenko went so far as to say that, 'Excessive monetary restrictions, that do not account for structural causes of inflation, may lead only to the reduction of output or to growth of non-payments ... reduced rates of monetary expansion in the second and third quarter of 1993 did not lead to a slowdown of inflation due to the non-monetary factors.'[4]

In the December 1993 elections the nationalists and the communists gained about 40% of the seats in parliament. The results of these elections should be interpreted as the logical sanction against the reformers, not for having gone too far with the reforms but for the opposite, for failure to deliver the most important of their promises: low inflation. Indeed, the second question of the April 1993 referendum, which concerned economic reform, received a positive response, indicating that the Russian people *en masse* approved of the reforms. The political importance of the inflation rate is revealed most graphically in the statistical manipulation of the April 1993 rate by order of the Chairman of the Supreme Soviet, Russian Khasbulatov.[5] At the time Goskomstat (the State Committee for Statistics) was, like the Central Bank, dependent on the Supreme Soviet. The reformers were arguing that, because of their policies, the rate of inflation was going down; Khasbulatov ordered Goskomstat to publish inflation figures closer to what he termed 'real life', in a change subsequently reversed after Khasbulatov and his clique were removed from power. As a result of the December elections, in January 1994 two out of the three leading reformers in the government, Boris Fyodorov and Yegor Gaidar, resigned, while Gerashchenko kept his position until 'Black Tuesday' (11 October 1994), which saw the external value of the rouble fall by 27% in a single day.

The CBR and its Supreme Soviet patrons were not solely responsible for the lack of control over the rate of inflation. The key factor, and the precondition for high inflation, was the high government budget deficit, largely financed in 1993 and 1994 by credits from the CBR. The experience of 1994 may be attributed to the destructive residual influence of the old

Central Bank–Supreme Soviet crediting system. The seasonal demands of the agricultural sector and of deliveries to the uneconomic far northern settlements deflected the government from its relatively tight monetary policy of the first half of 1994, and induced it to resort again to granting credits. The fact that the Central Bank was now more or less under government control in providing these credits, as it had in the previous two years, did not change the objective result: a surge of inflationary pressures and expectations. In the autumn of 1994, a new factor intervened to correct the situation, just as dramatically, in its way, as Yeltsin's dissolution of parliament a year earlier. By mid-1994 some effective financial markets had emerged, and on 11 October the Moscow foreign exchange market, bloated with excess roubles, passed judgment on the government's recent monetary and fiscal policies. The fall in the rouble exchange rate against the US dollar on this 'Black Tuesday' sparked a political crisis and government reshuffle, leading to a strong renewed commitment by Chernomyrdin and his ministers to a pro-stabilization strategy. In this sense, market forces (literally – the forces of financial markets) had developed sufficiently over three years to exert a decisive influence on the government and impel it to resume its drive towards monetary stabilization. This must be counted a remarkable success of economic transformation, where the effect of market-oriented reforms replaces a vicious circle with a virtuous one.

This survey of the Russian reformers' protracted struggle with inflation raises the question of the damage done by inflation. Some might argue that reforming energies would be better directed elsewhere. But while financing growth by inflationary means can be quite tempting politically, the possibility of stimulating growth by this means is limited. 'In the long run, one would expect an economy to adjust to whatever rate of monetary growth it experiences largely through price movements or conversely to adjust its monetary growth to its growth and price trends depending on whether its exchange rate is variable or fixed' (Johnson, 1965, p. 282). In practice, inflationary financing will retard economic growth by distorting the allocation of resources, 'by increasing uncertainty and reducing incentives for innovation and improvement' (Johnson, 1965, p. 291). In economies in transition, inflation, because of the associated uncertainty and relative price variability, is translated into extra output loss from diversion of real resources to speculative activity. Moreover, private investors do not find the uncertain environment of extreme inflation very conducive to new ventures. Above all, ordinary Russians have sought to evade the 'inflation tax' by fleeing the national currency and converting their savings into dollars. Inflation has therefore prevented the mobilization of domestic savings to cover the budget deficit and fund investment.

The remainder of this book is structured as follows. Chapter 1 analyses the legacy, both economic and political, bequeathed to Russia by the former regime. On the political side, the reforming government had to operate for two years under a Soviet constitution which vested undivided power in the Congress of People's Deputies – a body opposed to fundamental change in state and society alike. Chapter 2 studies the price liberalization begun on 2 January 1992 and shows that it did not go far enough, especially in failing to liberalize energy prices. Chapter 3 concentrates on the question of monetary stability, evaluating monetary policy and showing that at no time between 1992 and 1994 was there a tight monetary stance. Chapter 4 assesses the importance of external finance through an examination of the way the budget deficit was financed. Chapter 5 looks at the relationship between monetary expansion and the behaviour of the exchange rate. It shows that despite persistent systemic failures on the macroeconomic side, by 1994 Russia had reached the stage where the exchange rate responded to financial policies, making the threat of financial crisis on the exchange market a deterrent to lax monetary policy.

1 THE POLITICAL AND ECONOMIC LEGACY, 1980–91

'Do you often have queues as long as these?
No, not very often. Only when there
are goods in the shops.'

POLISH HUMOUR[1]

The communist regime in Russia came to an end with the dissolution of the Communist Party of the Soviet Union following the failed coup of August 1991, itself preceded by the proclamation on 12 June 1990 of the sovereignty of the Russian Soviet Federated Socialist Republic (RSFSR). 'On 8 December 1991, in Minsk, the RSFSR, Ukraine and Belarus entered into an agreement that called for the creation of a Commonwealth of Independent States (CIS) and declared that the USSR had ceased to exist; also in December 1991, a decree by the Russian President changed the country's official name from the RSFSR to the Russian Federation. Following the resignation from office of the President of the USSR (25 December, 1991), the Russian Federation has claimed successor status to the USSR as a subject of international law, including membership in international organisations.' (International Monetary Fund, 1992a, p. 1)

On 15 November 1991 the Russian government passed a 'package of fundamental legislation to provide a basis for radical economic and social change in the RSFSR', most of these measures following up commitments made by Yeltsin in his speech to the Russian Congress of People's Deputies on 28 October 1991. In February 1992 a more comprehensive programme was adopted, broadly similar to those previously launched in Poland and the former CSFR.[2] The opening phase of the economic reform programme in Russia involved price liberalization, increases in almost all the remaining administered prices, a more market-oriented dual foreign exchange market, and decrees on privatization of small-scale enterprises and agricultural land.

This chapter analyses the economic legacy which the former regime left Russia. This included:

- a budget deficit for 1991 estimated to be about 16.5% of GDP, financed exclusively by money creation;
- a monetary overhang in which M2 (defined as rouble currency plus rouble deposits) rose to around 77% of GDP in 1991;[3]
- an external debt estimated at around $67 billion at the end of 1991, with GDP at the end of 1991 estimated at R1,300 billion at the end of 1991;[4]
- almost no foreign exchange reserves.[5]

1.1. The pre-reform background

The Soviet planned economy was established in its definitive form in the 1930s. It was founded on the objective of achieving rapid industrialization by redirecting the factors of production from agriculture to industry. Private ownership was illegal, as was most economic activity not foreseen by the state plan. The emphasis was put on physical flows, leaving little role for prices.

Between 1960 and 1980 the retail price index (RPI) stayed almost constant, reflecting price controls (Cottarelli and Blejer, 1992). The RPI measured the price in the official market and takes into account only the state retail trade. Official statistics indicate that between 1960 and 1985 prices grew by less than 0.25% a year on average (Popov, 1994, p. 4), while non-official statistics give an estimate of between 1% and 3% a year.

1.2. The Soviet economy from maturity to decrepitude, 1980–85

Prior to the reforms introduced in 1987–8 (which transformed the mono-lithic banking system into a two-tier system), the functions of Gosbank (the state bank) covered both those of a central bank properly speaking and also those of commercial banks. There were exceptions: international reserves were managed by the Bank for Foreign Trade (Vnestorgbank); savings by Sberbank (which means literally 'savings bank'); and construction by Stroibank (i.e. the construction bank).

The Central Bank, which after the revolution of 1917 was only re-established in 1921 when it was subordinated to the Department of Finance (Popov, 1994), was responsible for the allocation of liquidity and credit resources. It was both 'banker to the government and lender to the enterprise sector' (IMF, 1992b, p. 3). Financial flows were divided between firms and

Figure 1.1. Soviet production: annual average rate of growth

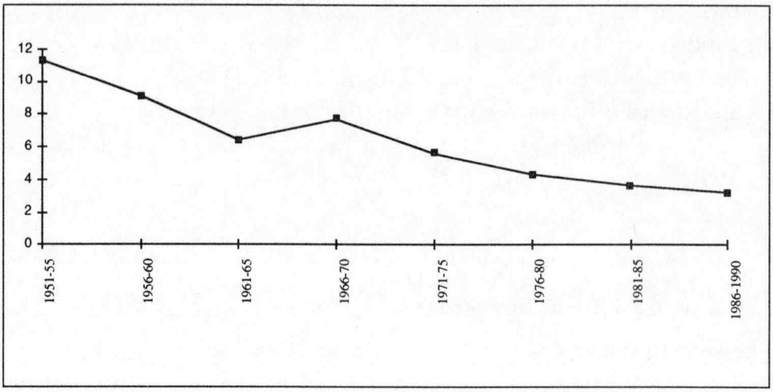

Source: Appendix 1, Table A.1.

households according to the credit plan and the cash plan respectively (IMF, 1992b). This dichotomy led to two forms of means of payment: cash for households and non-cash for enterprises. Credit allocation and the holding of deposits, for both enterprises and households, were likewise centralized under the control of the Gosbank. Monetary and fiscal policies were subordinated to the plan, which was executed by state enterprises supervised by sectoral branch ministries representing 90% of production (IMF et al., 1990, p. 3). Serious fiscal imbalances were avoided until the beginning of the 1980s.

Producer prices were fixed for long periods and consumer prices also varied little; such variations as there were bore no mutual relation. By introducing various taxes and subsidies according to the priorities of the plan at particular times (e.g. the 'price equalization' system), the authorities were able to isolate the economy from the world, reducing the role of the exchange rate to an accounting instrument. Foreign trade was centralized, with imports and exports decided on the basis of the strategic priorities of the plan.

In the early postwar period the system generated rapid growth; however, it was clear by the mid-1980s that, despite previous attempts at piecemeal reform (most notably in the late 1960s by the Soviet Prime Minister Kosygin, advised by Abel Aganbegyan), the limit had been reached (see Figure 1.1 above). Decentralization and partial reform started to take place in an effort to revive the system.

1.3. Economic perestroika, 1986–90

In 1985 the USSR embarked on an 'acceleration policy' similar to that pursued in Poland in the 1980s. Aimed mainly at the ageing machinery sector, it consisted of a series of *ad hoc* reforms, known as 'campaigns' (IMF et al., 1990, p. 3), designed to solve specific problems but lacking any strategic goal. These 'campaigns' included promotion of investment, quality control and the accountability of the bureaucracy; and the anti-alcohol campaign, which alone is said to have cost R10 billion in budget receipts (Zhukov, 1993, p. 3). The ideological principles of the planned economy were not challenged. This period of 'campaigns' lasted until about 1988.

These measures had no positive effect, and the economic situation deteriorated, leading to a new series of reforms designed to improve the system itself. The main development at this stage was the introduction of the law on state enterprises (1988), which gave these a measure of freedom over production and sales decisions. This law 'replaced traditional mandatory output targets for enterprises with so-called state orders (namely centrally directed orders to firms to deliver specified quantities of goods). The law also permitted firms some latitude to negotiate with each other, and granted them greater autonomy in the allocation of their internally generated funds, in particular, in the payment of wages and bonuses.' (IMF et al., 1990, p. 4) Workers were allowed to create private cooperatives and to lease capital from their enterprises; these quasi-private organizations accounted for 5% of employment by the end of 1990 (Murphy et al., 1992, p. 889). 'Encouragement of private economic activity was limited to small numbers of joint ventures with foreign participation and a grudging acceptance, beginning in 1988, of so-called co-operatives, which were, however, subject to various restrictions and sporadic campaigns of harassment.' (IMF et al., 1990, p. 4) However, while state enterprises had more freedom over their output, the centre sought to retain its powers by maintaining regulation over most prices: 'From 1988, enterprises were allowed to negotiate "contract" prices for so-called new products, but these were still subject to official surveillance and, in any event, covered only a fraction of enterprise production.' (IMF et al., 1990, p. 4) In consequence, resources moved to the private sector where prices were not controlled. This intensified the shortages in the state sector and contributed to the fall of 'measured' output (Murphy et al., 1992).

Reform in the foreign trade sphere was also undertaken; but here too it was only partial and failed to achieve the desired effects (IMF et al., 1990, p. 4). As well as decentralization of foreign trade, a foreign exchange retention scheme, a system of differentiated exchange coefficients and foreign currency auctions with limited transactions were introduced. But while imports in convertible currencies increased substantially following the decentralization of foreign trade, exports of manufactured products hardly changed.

Banking reform was attempted in 1988 with the introduction of a two-tier system. Three specialist state banks were created to channel credits and deposits to enterprises in the agriculture, industry and social investment sectors respectively (IMF, 1992b). The 1988 law on cooperatives permitted the creation of cooperative banks to service the newly created cooperatives not serviced by the state banks. The Gosbank remained untouched. No market disciplines were attached to credit allocation (which was direct), and interest rates remained low (and were themselves frequently reduced in various types of concessional lending).

To sum up, the years 1988–9 clearly showed how important it is when relaxing administrative controls in a command economy to introduce market-based controls in their place. This substitution was completely lacking in the reforms as they affected enterprises. As a result of the law on state enterprises, directors acquired freedom to increase wages without being subject to any real financial discipline (the so-called 'hard budget constraint') or price signals. Instead, they were able to finance increased wages with soft loans from the banking system and subsidies from the state budget. From 1988 to 1990, nominal wages grew much faster than the retail price index. In 1990, average real wages were 27% higher than their 1987 level (see Table 1.1).

In 1990, the Soviet economy entered a major crisis: output declined sharply, financial imbalances increased and external creditworthiness was cast into doubt. The budget deficit had started to grow out of control in 1986 (Sachs, 1994b) owing to the fall of world oil prices and to the increase in investment expenditures. According to Lin (1993, p. 369), during 1985–9 the budget deficit rose from about 2% to 9–10% of GNP. This contributed substantially to the 1990 crisis. During the 1980s the Soviet Union had financed the budget deficit through loans from international markets and governments (keeping the monetary financing of the deficit to low levels),

Table 1.1. Average nominal and real wages in Russia, 1987–90 (period average, in roubles)

		Nominal wage		Real wage[a]	
	R/m	% change	w/p	% change	RPI[b]
1987	216		100		1.6
1988	235	9	108.58	9	0.2
1989	259	10	116.86	8	2.4
1990	297	15	126.9	9	5.6

[a] The real wage is defined as the nominal wage in roubles deflated by the retail price index (RPI): w/p

[b] State stores and consumer cooperatives index through 1989, consolidated RPI for 1990.

Sources: Goskomstat; Koen and Phillips (1993), Table 6, p. 37.

but this raised the external debt from $20 billion in 1985 to $67 billion at the end of 1991. Sachs (1994b, p. 22) notes that in order to help maintain creditworthiness the sale of gold reserves was hidden.

The 'USSR Presidential Guidelines for the Stabilization of the Economy and Transition to a Market Economy' (16 October 1990) described the situation as follows: 'The position of the economy continues to deteriorate. The volume of production is declining. Economic links are being broken. Separatism is on the increase. The consumer market is severely depressed. The budget deficit and the solvency of the government are now at critical levels. Antisocial behaviour and crime are increasing. People are finding life more and more difficult and are losing their interest in work and their belief in the future.' (quoted in Osband, 1992a, p. 673)

1.4. 1991: slump

The situation deteriorated further in 1991. Trade collapsed as a result of the breakdown of the CMEA (exports to the CMEA declined from $35.5 billion in 1990 to $15.5 billion in 1991: see Table 1.4) and, following the failed coup in August, of the disintegration of the Soviet Union (see IMF et al., 1990, p. 11).[6]

In 1991, the budget deficit reached an extraordinary peak of 16.5% of GDP.[7] The main reasons for the deficit were:

Table 1.2. Russian GDP and NMP, 1991[a]

	Nominal GDP (Rbn)	Real GDP as % of previous year	NMP	Real NMP as % of previous year
1989	573.1		413	
1990	644		445	
1991	1,300	87.1	1051	86
1992	18,064	81.0	14652	78

[a] For definition of net material product see Appendix 1, Table A.1.
Source: Own calculations, data from Goskomstat RF, 1991–3, Russian Statistical Yearbook for 1990, 1991, 1992, Moscow, Russia (in Russian) and IMF (1995), Table 8, p. 70.

(1) the increase of state subsidies to support administratively controlled prices;
(2) the decline in output: Table 1.2 shows that real GDP declined by 13% between 1990 and 1991;
(3) the lack of tax discipline consequent on the break-up of the USSR and loss of payments from the republics.

During 1991 several ineffectual, if not actually damaging, reforms were undertaken. The first was the 'Pavlov reform'[8] of 22 January 1991, named after the Soviet prime minister who introduced it. This was an attempt to get rid of some of the monetary overhang by removing large-denomination (50- and 100-rouble) notes: about R4 billion were confiscated, 3% of the rouble money supply. The measure had almost no effect, apart from exciting popular discontent at arbitrary confiscation, because in practice virtually all holdings ended up by being converted into smaller-denomination rouble notes. It was intended to be a populist move, based on the general belief that large bank notes were earned illegally: but in the event it turned out to be deeply unpopular as it penalized many pensioners and other ordinary people who had built up large savings in these high-denomination notes. Secondly, an increase in producer and agricultural prices at the beginning of January 1991 was designed to raise incentives.

The January 1991 reform shifted many producer prices from the fixed to the contractual category. In theory, enterprises were permitted to negotiate contract prices of so-called new goods within administratively set limits. In practice, these prices reportedly were still heavily regulated and linked to state order prices. After the reform, contractual prices accounted for 40 per cent of the total in light industry, 50 per cent in machine construction, and about 25 per cent in the raw materials, energy and metals sectors. As before the reform, the prices of new products were allocated to be set on a contract basis. (Koen and Phillips, 1993, p. 2)

However, since retail prices were not changed before April 1991 the first effect of the reform was to increase the subsidy bill considerably.

To solve this problem, in April 1991 administered retail prices were increased by 60%. This measure 'reduced the share of fixed prices to 55 per cent in favour of regulated prices (15 per cent) and "contractual" prices between the producer and the retail unit (30%)' (Koen and Phillips, 1993, p. 3). The official policy was to compensate the population for 85% of the expected increase in expenditure resulting from the price reform and from index household deposits (as of March 1991) by 40%. Because of this level of compensation, increased tax collection was not enough to match price compensation payments and forgone profit taxes (IMF, 1992a, p. 12); the overall effect on the budget was therefore negative.

Before 1991, inflation as measured by the RPI was low (see Table 1.3). To a large degree, the monetary overhang was built up following the reform of state-owned firms. Managers and workers used this new flexibility to grant themselves large wage increases between 1988 and 1991. The 1991 price reforms at first slowed down this process, and in the second quarter of 1991 average real wages fell back to their 1987 level. But while retail prices remained more or less stable after the April 1991 reform, wages rose again, and by December 1991 amounted to twice their 1987 level: 'The national average wage rose 30 percent in the third quarter of 1991, reversing the recent real adjustment. In the final quarter of the year, retail price inflation accelerated to 16 percent, but was again outpaced by a 64 per cent surge in the average wage (73 percent in industry). By December 1991, statistical real wages were more than twice their 1987 levels. (This extreme outcome can be only partially explained by the seasonal bonus payments to wage earners in December.)' (Koen and Phillips, 1993, p. 15). With the loss of control over the increase in rouble wages (Commander, Liberman and Yemtsov, 1993, p. 16) excess demand developed while the price of state goods remained

Table 1.3. USSR yearly inflation rates, 1985–91 (%)

	1985	1986	1987	1988	1989	1990	1991
Wholesale industrial prices					1.2	3.9	138.1
Retail prices						5.6	90.4
Food	0.1	0.6	2.1	0.4	0.7	4.9	112.7
Alcoholic beverages	6.2	24.7	15.4			1.9	28.6
Non-food products	–0.9	–0.9	–1.1		3.1	6.5	100.7
Retail prices in:							
State and corporate trade	0.5	2.2	1.6	0.2	2.4	5.2	89.5
Cooperative trade	1.2	3.4	2.4	0.6	0.5	14.1	111.7
Collective farms	5.2	1.1	3.7	2.5	7.4	34.3	132.1

Source: IMF, Economic Review, *Russian Federation*, April 1992, p. 63.

controlled and worker productivity did not increase in line with wages: 'In the first six months of 1989 alone, the average monthly wages of workers and official salaries in the State sector increased by 10% while productivity increased by only 2.8%' (Linz, 1990, p. 12; see also Fender and Laing, 1992).

While there was little evidence of monetary overhang between 1964 and 1985 (Cottarelli and Blejer, 1992), during the perestroika period the overhang seems to have been huge. It was estimated to be equal to about nine months' earnings of the entire state sector workforce and in excess of the entire retail trade turnover in a single year (Linz, 1990, p. 12). As much as 25% of the waking time of every Soviet adult was spent in queues (Shleifer and Vishny, 1991; see also Fender and Laing, 1992). A black market existed, where prices were higher by 'up to five hundred percent' (Linz, 1990, p. 1).

The existence of a large monetary overhang allowed a much higher level of monetary financing by the Russian economy than in a market economy where consumers can easily escape inflation tax by diversifying their portfolio assets so that they can be taxed only on their desired monetary holdings:[9] in the case of the Soviet Union in the second half of the 1980s large monetary holdings could not be avoided. As a result, the ratio of financial assets to GDP rose from 30 per cent in the mid-1980s to 45 per cent by 1990 (World Bank, 1992, p. 12). In 1991, households paid 12% of GDP to the government through excess monetary holdings (World Bank, 1992, p. 11). This is very high by any standards; in cases of hyperinflation (Russia after the First World War; Poland, Hungary and Germany in the 1920s) the inflation tax was about

Table 1.4. Total Russian exports and imports ($bn)

	1990	1991[a]
Total exports	71.148	50.911
Per cent change[b]		39.75
Former socialist[c]	35.599	15.249
Developed economies	25.584	28.764
Developing economies	9.965	6.898
Total imports	81.751	44.473
Per cent change		83.82
Former socialist[c]	41.482	13.997
Developed economies	32.48	25.857
Developing economies	7.789	4.617

[a] See Havlik (1995), pp. 36–8, on the problems with Russian foreign trade statistics; and Kuboniwa (1995), pp. 47–50, on the reliability of foreign trade data for 1991.
[b] Percentage change over previous year.
[c] Estimated.

Sources: *RF v 1992 godu*, Moscow, Goskomstat RF, 1993, p. 50; Goskomstat RF, Ekonomicheskyi obzor, no.1, 1994, pp. 86–8; *Finansovye Izvestiya*, 28 April 1994, pp. I–II, quoted in Havlik (1995), Table 2.4, p. 32.

10–15% of GNP. The fact that the monetary overhang 'helped' the financing of the budget deficit in 1991 to such an extent may partly explain why the country was not driven to hyperinflation in the Cagan (1956) sense of the term (more than 50% per month).

Other factors in the deteriorating economic situation in 1991 included a sharp increase in inflation; and a decline in exports of 40% and in imports of 80% in US dollar terms (see Table 1.4). As already noted, the main decline was in exports to the CMEA, so the significance of this decline in trade may have been overstated: since the rouble was not convertible, a large part of these exports to the CMEA was in any case not going to be paid for. Also, much trade was conducted via unofficial channels. Nevertheless, at the end of 1991, foreign-exchange reserves were almost non-existent; and as a result of this shortage, foreign-exchange deposits (primarily of enterprises) held with the Vneshekonombank were frozen (IMF, 1992a, p. 21).

The only way to respond to such a catastrophic situation was to reduce the budget deficit and to end the situation of repressed inflation by liberalizing prices. The main cause of the prevailing economic chaos had been the fact that repressed inflation was no longer sustainable. However, flying in the face of this evidence, a good many Western experts attributed the whole situation to a 'production breakdown rather than a monetary breakdown' (Lipton and Sachs, 1992, p. 19);[10] and during the winter of 1991–2 fears of hunger were spread in the West, with the result that the Muscovites saw with great astonishment a huge operation called 'Food Aid' developed on their soil, led by a four-star German general.

2 PRICE LIBERALIZATION

Price liberalization in Russia started on 2 January 1992. The date of 16 December 1991 previously envisaged had been put back as a concession to Ukraine and Belarus, which requested more time to prepare themselves for this fundamental change. The irreversible character of price liberalization was demonstrated by an abortive measure attempted at the beginning of the Chernomyrdin administration in late December 1992 to reimpose administered prices.

However, price controls remained on food and energy despite Gaidar's determination to free these too;[1] and the resulting huge subsidies to these sectors were a major cause of the continuing budget deficit. The figures of 90% of consumer prices and 80% of producer prices freed in 1992 (Table 2.1) suggest a degree of price liberalization comparable to that achieved in Poland and the CSFR: but if calculated at free market prices rather than at 1991 prices it was significantly less: 'For example, housing rents – which typically represent a large share of consumer expenditure in market economies – were controlled and would thus be given in artificially low weight in such a calculation.' (Koen and Phillips, 1993, p. 4)

The initial jump in prices after the liberalization of 2 January 1992 was very large compared with those in Poland and the CSFR in the first month of their respective reform programmes (Table 2.2). In the case of Poland, the difference can be explained by the fact that 50% of Polish prices had already been liberalized in 1989 while, as we have seen, the April 1991 Soviet price reform was merely an increase in administered prices bearing no resemblance to a true price liberalization. In Russia, following the 2 January 1992 liberalization, producer prices rose by 382% and consumer prices by 296%.[2]

Various reasons can be advanced to explain the size of this initial price jump. First, it was exacerbated by the monetary overhang. The standard way of absorbing monetary overhang has been to inflate it away. This was certainly the case in Poland and also in Russia. With 296% inflation in January 1992

Table 2.1. Cross-country comparison of price liberalization (% of prices freed)

	Consumer prices	Producer prices
Poland 1990	83%	88%
CSFR 1991	90–95%	90–95%
Russia 1992	90%	80%

Source: Koen and Phillips (1993).

and a money supply growing on average between January 1992 and May 1992 at about 10% per month, the monetary overhang quickly disappeared. However, the question of price liberalization sweeping away savings needs further study: in 1991, whatever the amount of money one had, it was very difficult to find anything to buy; moreover, as a result of the privatization programme and of spontaneous privatization, many people found themselves owners of their apartments, which in many cases constituted an asset far more valuable than (although not as liquid as) the roubles held by households in saving accounts.

The second possible reason for the price jump was that the government's announcement that prices would rise by three to five times may have had an effect on expectations (Koen and Phillips, 1993, p. 6). Thirdly, the government embarked on price liberalization with a maximum 25% mark-up in the state distribution sector, shared between the wholesaler (19%) and the retailer (6%). This gave both producers and retailers a common interest in pushing prices as high as possible. The regulated prices prescribed by the authorities for certain basic foodstuffs were often ignored by producers. The government did not combat these violations; indeed, it lacked the administrative capacity to do so.

In the first wave of measures (January 1992), price regulation was maintained for energy resources (fuels, electricity), basic foodstuffs, precious metals, stones and freight tariffs. Fixed prices for basic fuels such as oil, oil products and coal were raised by approximately 400%; coking coal prices by 700%. The share of oil, gas and coal products allowed to be sold at free prices was increased, amounting to 40% by early May 1992 in the oil and gas sectors (Koen and Phillips, 1993, p. 4). In the foodstuffs sector, a limited number of goods were still regulated: bread, milk, sugar, vegetable oil, salt, vodka and

Table 2.2. Cross-country comparison of monthly rates of retail price inflation in the first, sixth and twelfth months after the beginning of price liberalization (%)

	Beginning of price liberalization	1st month	6th month	12th month
Poland	1st January 1990	79.6	3.4	5.9
CSFR	1st January 1991	25.8	1.8	1.2
Russia	2nd January 1992	296	13.9	25.1

Sources: Economic Commission for Europe (1992), Table 3.4.2, p. 93; Goskomstat.

baby food. But these accounted for no more than 5% of turnover. Moreover, the state distribution sector remained subject to a ceiling on its mark-up ratio (usually 25%, but up to 45% in the far north sub-polar regions, generally known as the 'Northern Territories').

Those first days of price liberalization saw bare shelves and high prices (Granville, 1992, pp. 3–4). After two weeks, however, there was growing evidence that market forces were beginning to operate, albeit in the absence of the privatization of retail trade, which was due to start in the second quarter of 1992. In the food production sector, the most elementary market force – withdrawal of demand in the face of higher relative prices – began to hold back the initial price rises. Producers responded to this fall in demand as a result of excessive initial price rises. In Yaroslavl, for instance, a 60-tonne consignment of dairy produce, which consumers refused to purchase at the new prices, was sent back to the producer factory for repricing. Having initially refused to compromise, the factory management offered the products to shops several days later at significantly reduced wholesale prices. Prices for some foods (meat, vegetable oil, butter, eggs) experienced a downward trend (Table 2.3).

Such initial market-type responses were complemented in some cases by local administrative measures. In some areas, the local authorities suppressed the 25% mark-up; in Kirov this measure resulted, for example, in a 33% fall in the price of chickens. Local authorities also intervened to enforce controlled prices. In Vladimir and Nizhny Novgorod, for example, protests against high milk prices led to such intervention, with a resultant fall in the price of a litre from 6 to 1.2 roubles and from 8.5 to 1.62 roubles respectively.

Table 2.3. Free food prices in Russia, January–March 1992 (R/kg, R/l)

	21 January 1992	25 February 1992	10 March 1992
Beef	83.9	69.48	52.08
Pork	82.69	73.93	—
Vegetable oil	29.85	23.31	19.46
Butter	114.34	82.76	88.5
10 eggs	17.39	14.86	—

Source: March 1992, Delovoi Mir (Business World).

After two months, the remaining regulated prices were again creating shortages of the products concerned.[3] Maintenance of these regulated prices required continuing large subsidies, especially with high inflation still running at 27.3% a month in February. As these subsidies were not forthcoming, the products in question began to disappear from the market, while supplies of freely priced products were plentiful – milk, for instance, disappeared while yoghurt and cheese remained widely available. Also, the price ceilings retained for several food items were exceeded in many cities from February 1992 onwards. The number of cities in which ceilings were exceeded increased in early February, with, for instance, 39 cities out of 130 sampled reporting vegetable oil sales above the price limit on 11 February.[4] Consequently the federal government decided to free the remaining controlled prices on food products (including central controls on retail bread prices), although some local authorities elected to keep them (see Table 2.4). This second wave of liberalization came in March–April 1992 (Koen and Phillips, 1993, p. 4), leaving administered prices only for rents, utilities, public transport and energy, and wholesale state grain purchases.

The third wave was supposed to include energy prices, but the timing and scope of fuel price liberalization remained highly controversial. It was feared that energy price liberalization would not only cause a sharp increase in inflation but also reduce the production of food and consumer goods. Worries about the effect on the harvest and therefore on the price of bread were paramount. So, instead of applying full liberalization, on 18 May 1992 the government raised the wholesale price of crude oil from R350 per tonne to R2,200 per tonne. This was about $20 at the exchange rate on 20 May 1992 (R113: US$1), with the world price at the time standing at about $120. But

Table 2.4. Controls on food prices in Russia, mid-1992 (%)

Product	Proportion of cities in which price remained controlled[a]	Product	Proportion of cities in which price remained controlled[a]
Milk	44	Top quality wheat bread	10
Kefir	36	Sugar	30
Fat cottage cheese	29	Salt	17
Rye bread	30	Meat products	11
Mixed rye-wheat bread	28	Butter	6
Grade 1 and 2 wheat bread	32	Vegetable oil	14

[a] Sample of 132 cities.
Source: Goskomstat, quoted in Koen and Phillips (1993), Table 9, p. 41.

at the same time the right of producers to sell a proportion of their production at a price exceeding the administrative ceiling was abolished.

It was a serious mistake to maintain energy price controls (Lipton and Sachs, 1992, p. 22) since higher prices would have depressed domestic demand and made it possible to export more oil and gas and so earn greatly needed revenues. The failure to liberalize energy prices was based on the mistaken premise that the increase in energy prices would be inflationary. The authorities failed to see that the rise in prices entailed by liberalization would cause only a temporary increase in inflation, which would soon have returned to its previous level. Indeed, one can go further than this. Higher energy prices would have decreased the budget deficit and therefore reduced the need for monetary financing. The result would have been lower inflation, with the exception of a one-month jump in the overall price level. Instead, the low price of energy meant huge subsidies to the energy sector and lost revenue as a result of artificially depressed prices.

The absence of any lasting connection between energy price formation and inflation is illustrated by Figure 2.1, which compares the paths of coal prices and inflation. We can see that while in May 1992 the price of coal rose from R157/tonne to R653/tonne, inflation was relatively stable between May 1992 and August 1992 at about 10% due to the relatively low monetary growth in the early months of 1992. We can generalize this result by comparing the consumer price index (CPI) with an index of energy price increases (Berg et al., 1993).[5] There were three important increases in the

Figure 2.1. Inflation and variation of coal prices in Russia, January 1992–June 1993

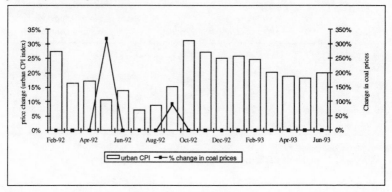

Source: Berg and Delpla (1993), p. 4.

price of energy with the sharpest rise in May 1992, when the price of gas rose by 419%, of oil by 471% and of coal by 316%, and the overall energy price index by 415%. If we compare this energy price increase with the CPI we find that from May to August 1992 the rate of inflation did not accelerate but slackened. To go further, the relationship between the CPI and the energy price index was statistically tested. Monthly inflation (DCPI) was regressed on energy price inflation (DEPR) with different lags of one, two, three and four months. In no case was the relationship statistically significant.[6]

Since the fundamental price liberalization of 1992, the federal government has continued to maintain various price controls, either directly, as for public utilities, or else via profit margins (limited to a fixed percentage of the production costs)[7] and export quotas on oil and oil products. These price controls were largely ineffective, especially in the case of petrol, causing sales to be diverted from the state market, with petrol being sold direct from tankers on street corners at substantially higher prices than in state petrol stations. The quota system was replaced with quarterly government-approved export allocations by a government resolution signed by Chernomyrdin on 31 December 1994, enforcing a presidential decree to lift oil export quotas as of 1 January 1995.[8] The freeing of the oil price will have a beneficial impact on inflation since tax revenues will further increase because export taxes are calculated according to the per tonne price of crude oil on the domestic market. If the same excise tax were to be assessed on a domestic price that was closer to international prices, it would greatly improve the budget.

Indeed, the consequences for the budget of those price controls were enormous. If the level of the initial price jump in Russia was exacerbated by the existence of monetary overhang,[9] the subsequent high inflation rates were due to the fiscal and quasi-fiscal expenditures and the way they were financed. Inflation stayed so high after the initial jump not because of price liberalization but because monetary policy was loose; and one of the reasons for that monetary laxity was the effect on the budget deficit of subsidies arising from the remaining price controls.

3 MONETARY POLICY

In the 'Guidelines on the monetary policy of the CBR' presented to the Russian parliament at the beginning of March 1992, the Gaidar government committed itself to quarterly target growth rates. This, together with a broadly balanced budget for 1992 and confidence in the rouble, was to have created the necessary conditions for monetary stability.

The targets were aimed at reducing the M2 growth rate as follows: for the first quarter (Q1) of 1992, by 25–30%; Q2 1992, 15–30%; Q3 1992, 5–20%; and Q4 1992, 0–10%. This means that for Q1 1992, for instance, the monthly inflation rate should not have exceeded 10%. The annualized growth of M2 for 1992 should have been between 50% and 120%.[1] Figure 3.1, which takes the monthly average of these quarterly targets and compares them with the actual monthly increase of M2, shows that the monthly increase far exceeded the agreed targets, especially from June 1992. The result was high inflation during the whole of 1992 and 1993. One extenuating factor in this failure was the total disorder of monetary data, which made such targets unreliable.

3.1. The link between CBR credits, the money supply and inflation

From the quantity theory equation, prices may increase as a result of a growth of the money supply, an increase in the velocity of money, or a decline of output, assuming in each case that the other two factors remained unchanged. In practice, changes in the other two factors may either reinforce or offset the initial disturbance.

Causes of the growth in money supply
To understand the factors at the origin of the increase in the money supply, it is necessary to consider the balance sheet of the Central Bank of Russia (see Table 3.1). From the balance sheet we can see the relation between the monetary base and domestic credits. A change in the monetary base is given by:

Figure 3.1. Russia: actual monetary growth compared with original targets in 1993

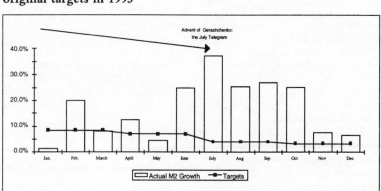

Source: Appendix 1, Table A.2.

$$(3.1) \quad \Delta MB = \Delta NIR + \Delta NCG + \Delta GCB + \Delta NCFSR + \Delta OIN$$

and domestic credits, which is the change in net domestic assets, by:

$$(3.2) \quad \Delta CE = \Delta NCG + \Delta GCB + \Delta NCFSR = \Delta MB - \Delta NIR - \Delta OIN$$

This shows that the growth of the money supply through the money multiplier depends on three types of Central Bank credits:

(1) ΔNCG: net credit to the government, i.e. the monetary financing of the budget deficit.

(2) ΔGCB: gross credits to commercial banks. In 1993, the IMF advised the CBR to change its methodology slightly and count net credits (that is gross credits minus excess reserves) rather than gross credits to commercial banks. These credits were not confined to providing liquidity to banks through the refinance rate; they also comprised subsidized credits funded by the budget and the Central Bank and channelled through commercial banks to state enterprises.

(3) $\Delta NCFSR$: net credit to former Soviet republics (FSRs). In 1992 and 1993 the CBR provided non-cash and cash credits to the 'near-abroad' countries

Table 3.1. Balance sheet of the Central Bank of Russia

Assets	Liabilities

NIR: net international reserves
   GIR: gross international reserves
− GIL: gross international liabilities:
	MB: monetary base
	   Cash issued
	+ Required reserves of the commercial
	   banks
	+ Excess reserves of the commercial banks

NDA: net domestic assets
   NCG: net credit to government*
+ GCB: gross credit to commercial banks
+ NCFSR: net credit to former Soviet
   republics
 	
+ OIN: other items net	

Total assets	Total liabilities

* Net credit to government = credits to government minus government deposits.

to allow their enterprises to continue trading with Russian enterprises. Credits to FSRs financed these countries' imports from Russia and thus had much the same effect as direct subsidies to Russian industries, the main difference being that with pure subsidies the products may not even be sold but simply pile up at the factory. At the same time the FSRs' central banks were themselves able to issue rouble credits to be spent in Russia, thus further contributing to the growth of Russia's money supply and inflation (Granville, 1992, 1994). While non-cash credit started to be regulated in July 1992, cash credit was not. In 1993, since transfers in cash were not regulated, the Central Bank, still under the control of the Supreme Soviet, saw the opportunity to make transfers in cash in the form of pre-1993 banknotes, i.e. those not carrying the Russian flag. The use of cash was, however, abruptly stopped in July 1993 with the removal from circulation of the pre-1993 rouble notes (Granville, 1994; Popov, 1994). Such transfers epitomized the conflict between the Ministry of Finance and the CBR. The conflict came to a head in 1993, when the Ministry under Boris Fyodorov was trying to cut these credits to FSRs while the CBR aimed to continue financing enterprises in the 'near abroad'. The details of this conflict will not be recounted in detail here.

Table 3.2. Total quarterly CBR credit as % of quarterly GDP, end of quarter, 1992–4

Quarter	Total	Budget[a]	GCB[b]	NCB[c]	FSR[d]	GDP[e]
1992						
Q1	6.00%	−6.11%	9.93%	7.31%	2.18%	1831.9
Q2	43.83%	25.24%	8.63%	−3.65%	9.95%	2733
Q3	26.02%	9.42%	14.10%	−1.15%	2.49%	5042.2
Q4	26.20%	2.09%	18.57%	10.27%	5.53%	8457.4
Year	30.13%	9.37%	15.74%	4.52%	5.01%	18064.5
1993						
Q1	11.68%	0.07%	6.57%	6.97%	5.03%	15801
Q2	2.66%	−3.45%	5.05%	4.85%	1.06%	30012
Q3	19.59%	12.53%	5.94%	2.54%	1.12%	44140
Q4	8.64%	7.80%	0.99%	−0.84%	−0.15%	72391
Year	14.16%	7.30%	5.38%	1.89%	1.48%	162344
1994						
Q1	6.63%	4.78%	1.82%	4.07%	0.01%	94200
Q2	10.39%	7.75%	2.71%	1.06%	−0.08%	141300
Q3	14.07%	11.68%	2.43%	0.47%	−0.04%	167600

[a] Net credit to government, which includes federal government, local government, and extra-budgetary funds.

[b] Gross credits to commercial banks, including excess reserve credits. This means that the monetary base should be calculated in its broad definition with excess reserves deposits at the central bank.

[c] Net credit to commercial banks, i.e. excluding excess reserve credits; at this time the monetary base should be calculated without excess reserves.

[d] Credit to former Soviet republics.

[e] Figures are in current prices from Goskomstat.

Source: calculated with data from CBR.

The Ministry of Finance was in essence forced to exercise responsibility for monetary policy when this rested properly with the Central Bank, which however preferred to create money to shelter the economy from market forces.

Total CBR credit flows per quarter as a percentage of GDP accelerated sharply in the second quarter of 1992 and then declined substantially in the third quarter of 1993 and first quarter of 1994 before picking up in the third quarter of 1994 (see Table 3.2 and Figure 3.2).

Figure 3.2. Quarterly CBR credits as a percentage of GDP

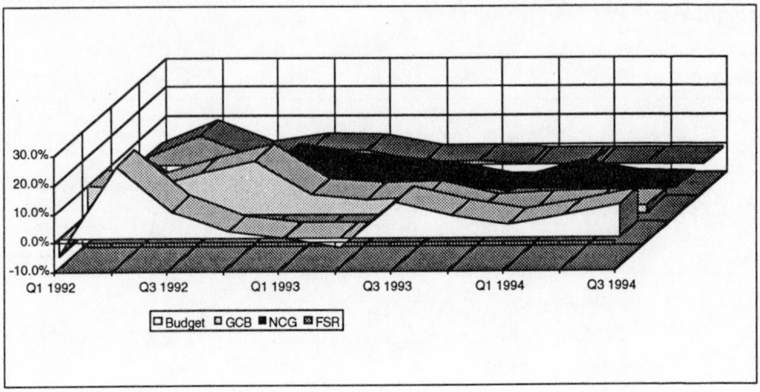

Source: Table 3.2.

Chapter 4 will study in more detail the credits to the budget and the gross credits to commercial banks which can be used as a proxy for directed credits (IMF, 1995, p. 32).

The next relationship of significance is that between the monetary base created by the Central Bank and the level of the broad money supply held by the public (M2). The Central Bank directly determines the level of the monetary base (MB), which equals commercial bank reserves plus cash issued by the Central Bank (M0). The relation between the monetary base and M2 depends on the reserve requirement ratio, the amount of excess reserves held by commercial banks at the Central Bank, interest rates, and the efficiency of the payments system. The ratio of M2 to MB is the money multiplier $K = M2/MB$, where M2 is defined as currency outside banks plus rouble deposits (i.e. demand deposits plus time and saving deposits) and MB is the monetary base, equal to required reserves plus excess reserves of the commercial banks and total currency issued by the central bank.

The money multiplier fell sharply at the start of 1992 when reserve requirements were raised, and it has fluctuated quite widely since then (see Figure 3.3). Reserve requirements were increased at the beginning of 1992 from 2% to 15% on short-term deposits (less than one year) and 10% on longer-term deposits. In April 1992, the requirements were raised to 20% and 15% for short- and long-term deposits respectively. But this rather high requirement of 17.5% on average was not enforced, as revealed by the actual

Figure 3.3. Money multiplier and excess reserves ratio, December 1991–December 1994

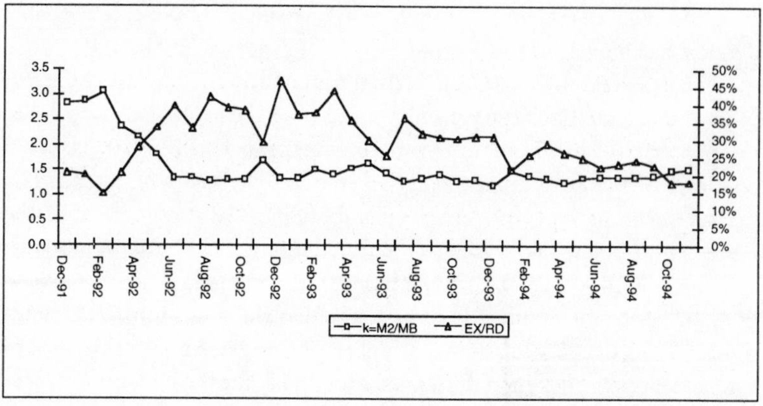

Source: Appendix 1, Tables A.2 and A.4.

reserve deposit ratio which amounted to no more than 11% at the end of December 1992 (Appendix 1, Table A.4). Although there is no obvious explanation for this difference between the minimum reserve requirement imposed by law and the actual reserves held by banks, various hypotheses may be advanced. First, the method by which reserve requirements were calculated entailed a certain amount of fraud and miscalculation. As the IMF (1995, p. 202) noted:

> With the permission of the CBR, commercial banks can choose the deposit base on which reserve requirements are calculated from two different methods: (1) the average of the balances at the end of consecutive 5 day periods each month; (2) the average on daily balances for all days in the month. In addition, all banks are required to provide deposit balances on the first day of the month. Provision of deposit balances relating to the 16th day of the month is optional. This method allows for two or more banks to collude in shifting deposits in order to obtain a more favourable (lower) reserve requirement.

The fact that the calculation took place only once a month gave even more opportunity of collusion and fraud to commercial banks. The method was eventually changed in 1995. Second, there was no required minimum reserve on centralized credits, which meant that 30–50% of these were not covered (Fyodorov, 1994, p. 4). However, in 1994 the minimum requirement was more or less enforced, with the ratio of minimum reserve to rouble deposits reaching 17.2% in October 1994 (Appendix 1, Table A.4).

The main reason for the changes in the money multiplier during the first years of transition lay in the behaviour of commercial banks' excess reserves, due in part to the inefficiency of the payment system. The IMF (1993a, p. 26) confirms the link between the excess reserves and the payment system: 'The measurement of base money is difficult in Russia, partly because the settlement of interbank payments is effected through the CBR interbranch clearing system. As a consequence, commercial banks hold balances in excess of required reserves at the CBR to meet settlement obligations.' Rising for most of 1992, excess reserves in December 1992 reached no less than 47% of rouble deposits. They then declined fairly steadily for the next two years to 18% at the end of November 1994 (Appendix 1, Table A.4).

In 1992 and early 1993 the relation between the money supply and prices was empirically straightforward (Figure 3.4). A four-month lag was observed between the rate of growth of M2 and that of prices. Some of the monthly jumps in the consumer price inflation curve correspond to the liberalization of administrative prices of energy, utilities, public transport and food products.

Table 3.3 shows the result of a regression of inflation (DCPI) on five lags of money growth (DM2) and a measure of real energy price changes (DEPR) from July 1992 to August 1993 (14 observations). Apart from the constant term, only the four-month lag of M2 growth is statistically significant, as indicated by its t-ratio of 2.8. None of the other lags are significant at the conventional levels. This is the basic evidence in support of the view that at this period of the Russian transition monetary transmission took four months.

Table 3.4 reruns this regression retaining only the four-month lag on M2 growth, i.e. DM2(–4). The estimated coefficient indicates that on average a 1% increase in M2 growth was associated with a 0.5% increase in prices four months later.

$$(3.3) \quad DCPI = 0.09 + 0.51 \times DM2(-4) + 0.06 \times DEPR$$
$$\qquad\qquad (3.61) \qquad (4.98) \qquad (1.00)$$
$$\qquad R^2 = 0.69$$

The t-statistics are in parentheses. The number of available observations is too small for strict interpretations of these t-statistics, but clearly M2 growth is a

Figure 3.4. Russia: consumer price inflation and rouble M2 growth, lagged 4 months

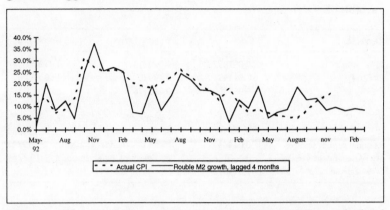

Source: This graph appears in various studies but the main source is Sachs (1993). It was developed in the MFU of the Ministry of Finance of the Russian Federation (dissolved in January 1994 when Anders Åslund and Jeffrey Sachs resigned as advisers to the Russian government).

Table 3.3. Money growth and consumer price changes, July 1992–August 1993: ordinary least squares estimation (dependent variable: DCPI)

Regressor	Coefficient	Standard error	t-ratio[prob.]
C	0.12883	0.048494	2.6567[.033]
DM2(−1)	−0.074536	0.090465	−0.82392[.437]
DM2(−2)	−0.17617	0.11587	−1.5205[.172]
DM2(−3)	0.16275	0.11777	1.3820[.209]
DM2(−4)	0.34856	0.12022	2.8992[.023]
DM2(−5)	0.13428	0.12365	1.0860[.313]
DEPR	0.1873E-3	0.071680	0.0026124[.998]
R^2	0.84498	F-statistic F(6, 7)	6.3592[.014]
R^{-2}	0.71210	SE of regression	0.032293
Residual sum of squares	0.0073000	Mean of dependent variable	0.19721
SD of dependent variable	0.060186	Maximum of log-likelihood	33.0474
DW-statistic[a]	1.3115		

[a] The DW-statistics are low in this regression, suggesting positive serial correlation; but further runs using the Lagrangian multiplier test of residual serial correlation did not provide evidence for serial correlation at the 5% level.

Table 3.4. Money growth and consumer price changes, July 1992–August 1993: ordinary least squares estimation (dependent variable: DCPI)

Regressor	Coefficient	Standard error	t-ratio[prob.]
C	0.092832	0.025713	3.6104[.004]
DM2(-4)	0.51449	0.10330	4.9805[.000]
DEPR	0.061322	0.060936	1.0063[.336]
R^2	0.69331	F-statistic F(2, 11)	12.4331[.002]
R^{-2}	0.63754	SE of regression	0.036235
Residual sum of squares	0.014442	Mean of dependent variable	0.19721
SD of dependent variable	0.060186	Maximum of log-likelihood	28.2714
DW-statistic	1.5138		

significant predictor of inflation. The measure of real energy price increase (DEPR) as an explanatory variable of inflation is insignificant statistically.

The relation between the growth of M2 (lagged four months) and the monthly inflation rate did not hold so clearly at the end of 1993. While M2 grew at an average rate of 17% for the first ten months of 1993, showing some tightening in the allocation of credits, the inflation rate grew faster. At the end of October 1993 it had again risen to about 20% monthly.

A large monetization of foreign assets was at work, due to the fact that in the first half of 1993 there was a large trade surplus and commercial banks responded to the credit tightening by moving some of their excess reserves on to the market. This trend slowed down in the second half of 1993, when Central Bank credit to the government was the main factor in monetary expansion (Table 3.5).

In 1994, the relation between M2 and the CPI became even looser (Figure 3.5), but in the opposite direction, with the growth of M2 on average higher than the increase in CPI. This reflected largely the decrease in monetary velocity which occurred in July and August 1994 (Appendix 1, Table A.2) as the inflation rate fell to 5.3% and 4.6% respectively.

Was velocity constant?
The velocity of money is defined as the ratio of nominal GDP (PQ) to the money supply (rouble M2). In other terms, velocity is the inverse of the ratio of M2 (in this case) to GDP. Increase/decrease in monetary velocity means

Table 3.5. Summary indicators of money and credit, 1993–4: quarterly changes (%)

	1993					1994
	QI	Q2	Q3	Q4	Year	QI
Within period changes in relation to monetary base at beginning of period						
Base money[a]	59	88	61	55	645	23
Net international reserves[b,c]	28	50	7	−1	122	−12
Net domestic assets[b,c]	30	38	54	56	523	35
of which:						
Net credit to the enlarged government	6	−29	83	51	452	38
Net credit to banks	13	41	17	−6	100	5
Interstate loans	36	9	9	−2	67	0
Other items (net)	−24	17	−55	13	−96	−8

[a] The fact that base money = NIR+NDA does not exactly add up is due to rounding.

[b] Change in relation to monetary base at the beginning of the period.

[c] Net international reserves of the monetary authorities. Calculated using average quarterly (where appropriate, annual) exchange rates.

Source: IMF (1995), Table 33, p. 94.

Figure 3.5. Forecasts of CPI according to rouble M2 (lagged 4 months), January 1994–March 1995

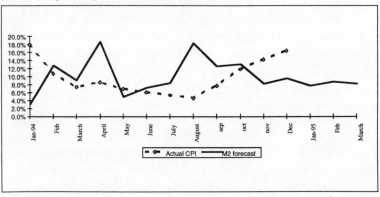

Source: Appendix 1, Table A.2.

Figure 3.6. M2 and M1 velocity

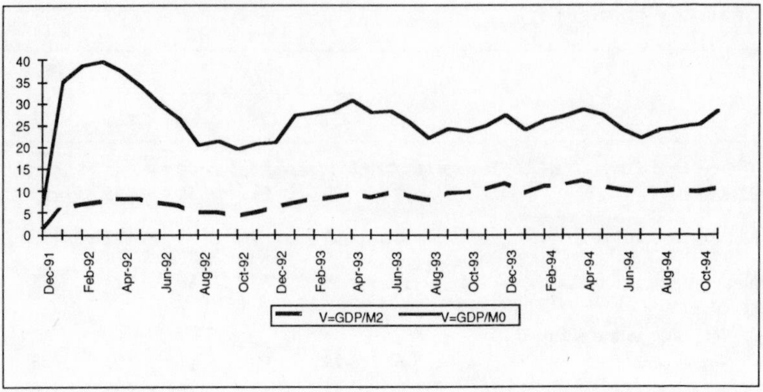

Sources: *Quarterly Bulletin* of the CBR; Goskomstat; Appendix 1, Table A.2.

that cumulative price increases are greater/smaller than cumulative increases in M2.

From December 1991 to January 1992 the income velocity (defined as annualized monthly GDP divided by end-of-period broad money) of rouble M2 (defined as currency outside banks plus rouble deposits) jumped from 1.3 to 6.4 due to the liberalization of prices (passage from repressed inflation to open inflation). It then accelerated in June 1992. Throughout 1992, 1993 and 1994 velocity varied widely. It is thus difficult to assume M2 velocity as a constant and so to rely on the strict quantity equation for Russia.

Rouble money (M2) as a share of (annual average) GDP decreased from 16% in January 1992 to 14% in January 1993 and 10% in November 1994. This is reflected in Figure 3.6, where substantial variations of velocity can be observed.

Various factors were at work here:

(1) The decline in velocity in the third and fourth quarters of 1992 can be explained by the ending of the cash shortage and the slowing down of the inflation rate to 17.2% in April 1992 from 27.3% in February 1992.
(2) Since there is a time lag between the injection of money into the economy and the behaviour of economic agents, the increase in income velocity during the fourth quarter of 1992 and especially the first quarter of 1993 may reflect this lag effect.

Figure 3.7. M2 velocity

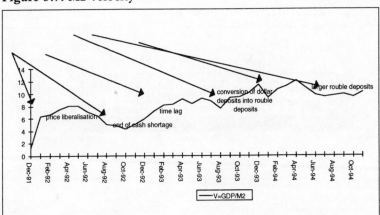

Source: Appendix 1, Table A.2.

(3) The increase in foreign-exchange deposits following the variation of the exchange rate reflected declining confidence in the rouble combined with strong expectations of further inflation. This helps to explain the jump in the first quarter of 1993 and the general increase during 1993, with a decline in August reflecting the conversion of dollar balances into rouble balances due to the appreciation of the rouble and the rise in domestic interest rates.

(4) Velocity was high in the first months of 1994 (Figure 3.7). In July 1994 and August 1994, M2 velocity decreased, suggesting that Russians had accumulated larger rouble deposits following the high real interest rates. Rouble deposits as a share of GDP varied widely over the period (Figure 3.8), while currency outside banks stayed relatively constant, suggesting that people needed broadly the same amount of currency for transactions while rouble deposits depended on the domestic interest rate, on the exchange rate and on the rate offered on foreign-exchange deposits.

As the increase in prices raised the transaction demand for money, negative rouble real interest rates discouraged rouble deposits and encouraged dollar deposits. Households reacted to the high inflationary environment and

Figure 3.8. Components of broad money as a percentage of yearly average GDP

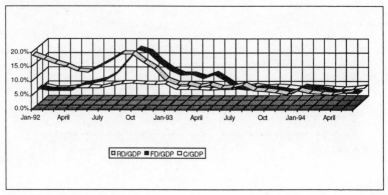

Source: Appendix 1, Table A.6.

to the low interest rate on saving deposits by reducing their deposits at the saving bank (Sberbank) from 5.9% of GDP in January 1992 to 1% in October 1993 (Figure 3.9). But from December 1993 to October 1994 saving deposits started rising as a result of high interest rates. (Deposits at the Sberbank are the only deposits guaranteed by the state.)

Enterprises responded similarly. Total rouble deposits (including those at the Sberbank) declined from 66% of broad money (that is M2 + foreign-exchange deposits) in January 1992 to 39% in June 1993 (Figure 3.10), before picking up during the summer as a result of the exchange-rate appreciation and the increased interest rate. Also, as explained for 1992 by Easterly and Vieira de Cunha (1993, p. 16):

> Enterprise flows with the real economy also seem to imply a relatively healthy bottom line. Gross profits (including depreciation) were 40 per cent of GDP for all enterprises. Fixed investment is estimated at 21 percent of GDP, not a catastrophic low by comparison with past years or international standards. There are no official figures yet on inventory accumulation for 1992, but the Russian Government's Centre for Economic Analysis and Forecasting makes a guess estimate of 9 percent of GDP. Inventory accumulation could be interpreted as the piling up of unsaleable output; however, it is just as plausible that enterprises found inventory accumulation attractive as an inflation hedge.

Figure 3.9. Russia: household deposits in Sberbank as percentage of GDP, 1992–4

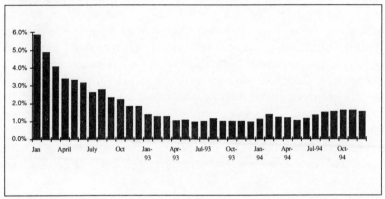

Source: Appendix 1, Table A.5.

Figure 3.10. Composition of money holdings, 1992–4

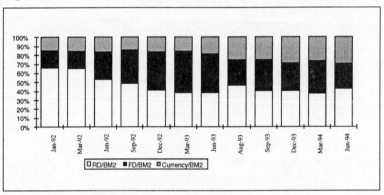

Source: Appendix 1, Table A.6.

Foreign-exchange deposits rose from 19% of total broad money in January 1992 to 43% in June 1993 before declining to 30% in August 1993, while the share of currency in broad money rose from 15% at the end of March 1992 to 29% in December 1993 (Figure 3.10). Wages were paid twice monthly, and because of the badly functioning banking system and system of payments, small businesses increasingly used cash.

3.2. Was monetary policy too tight?

Russia from 1992 to 1994 does not follow the credit crunch model of Calvo and Coricelli (1993). The view defended here is that the credit squeeze assumption had no reality in Russia and can be refuted on the following grounds. First, greatly increased yields from taxes on company profits and rapidly rising wages indicate that the liquidity squeeze has been overestimated (Appendix 1, Table A.8). Secondly, if we look at the level of real reserves we see that, contrary to the view of Ickes and Ryterman (1992, p. 18), these rose rapidly from April 1992 onwards and in October 1992 reached an extraordinary high (Figure 3.11).[2] While the minimum reserve requirement was 20% on short-term deposits and 15% on long-term deposits (of which there were hardly any), once excess reserves were taken into account the total reserve ratio amounted to 47.4% at the end of June 1992 and 49.2% at the end of August 1992.

It is especially hard to understand why banks held such an amount of excess reserves, which were non-interest-bearing, in the context of an average monthly inflation rate of around 25% in 1992, 20% in 1993 and 8% in 1994, which thus constituted a severe tax on bank asset earnings. Of course, much of this tax was shifted to depositors, resulting in their interest rates being probably much lower than would otherwise have been the case. Nonetheless, none of the various explanations of this phenomenon examined by Khoo and Tsepliaeva (1994) is very satisfactory.[3] Each explanation seems only partial, failing to account for aspects such as the weaknesses of the settlement system, and the poor ability of banks to manage their liquidity efficiently. Treasury bills – the only source of domestic interest-bearing reserves for commercial banks – were introduced only in May 1993, and then in a rather limited fashion.[4]

A further partial explanation of the high level of excess reserves is the existence of large credit risks. The following example demonstrates this effect.

Assuming no credit risk and profit-maximizing behaviour, banks would choose their desired level of excess reserves such that at the margin the expected value of a rouble withdrawn from the reserves and lent should equal the return obtained on this rouble if it were left in reserve. Assuming lending rates in July 1992 to be 120%, a penalty overdraft rate of 80% x 2 = 160% (which was at the time twice the Central Bank refinance rate), and zero interest on excess reserves:

$$(3.4) \qquad 0 = 120\% \star (1-p) + (120\% - 160\%) \star p$$

Figure 3.11. Real total reserves (deflated by the CPI, base: January 1992)

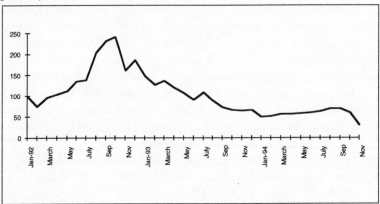

Source: Appendix 1, Table A.4.

p being the probability that the bank will find itself short of reserves. This gives:

$$(3.5) \qquad p = 3/4$$

In other words, assuming that the overdraft facility was unlimited, with no transaction costs, and that excess reserves were free reserves, banks would choose a level of excess reserves such that on three days out of four they would be short of reserves and use the overdraft facility. This confirms that the high level of excess reserves in the Russian monetary system could be due to high risks and institutional bottlenecks within the banking system.

Another explanation for the high level of excess reserves has to do with directed credits distributed by the CBR to firms through the major banks. These credits were substantial. Owing to the slow settlement system, they inflated the line 'correspondent accounts' which are assumed here to be mainly excess reserves but which also include these credits. Of course, if that was the main explanation for excess reserves, the multiplier should be calculated with the monetary base taking into account only the minimum reserve requirement. The IMF chose to apply this method in 1993. But even in a period of relative tightening of credits channelled through commercial banks, such as the last quarter of 1993 (see Table 3.2 above), the ratio of excess reserves on rouble deposits was still on average 30%. This suggests that directed credits were not the whole story, especially as banks could have made profits on the foreign-exchange market while waiting to channel these credits (see Chapter 5 below).

The high level of reserves in either nominal or real terms through 1992 and 1993 (Appendix 1, Table A.4) caused a risk of a new acceleration of the money supply, even in the absence of increased credits. The point is that given the large excess reserves held by commercial banks in their correspondent accounts at the CBR, changes in demand for excess reserves could create substantial movements in the money multiplier. In August 1993, for example, compulsory reserves stood at R1,615.1 billion while funds deposited in CBR correspondent accounts amounted to R4,407 billion (Appendix 1, Table A.4). This means that if all the banks with excess reserves had decided to use them at the same time to expand credit, the money supply could have increased by four times. Since the money multiplier is determined by the level of reserves, it increases if commercial banks withdraw reserves from the Central Bank; and, given the monetary base, the money supply increases with the multiplier. So the fall of reserves will raise the money multiplier and prices as well, although with a lag (Figure 3.12).

The refinance rate is the rate at which the CBR lends to commercial banks. In 1991, the State Bank of the former USSR (Gosbank) increased the refinance rate by several percentage points compared with 1990. The annual interest rate at which the commercial banks were allowed to borrow was then between 6% and 9% at the CBR, while it was about 12% at the Gosbank. At the beginning of 1992 the CBR rate was raised to 20%, in April to 50%, and in May to 80% (Appendix 1, Table A.3).[5] In response to pressure from the IMF the refinance rate was raised to 180% per annum in September 1993, then to 210%. The agreement with the IMF was that the refinance rate would not fall more than 7 percentage points below the interbank rate by 1 July 1993.[6] Table A.3, Appendix 1, shows the details of the various changes in the refinance rate during 1992–4. Not until November 1993 did the real refinance rate became positive at 0.9% monthly (Appendix 1, Table A.9).

Bank interest rates were freed at the end of 1991 for both deposits and loans, but they nevertheless remained negative in real terms in 1992 and for most of 1993. Table A.10 in Appendix 1 shows that the holding of interest-earning deposits was particularly unattractive. They followed the same development as the refinance rate.

Figure 3.12. Russia: money multiplier and total reserves deposit ratio

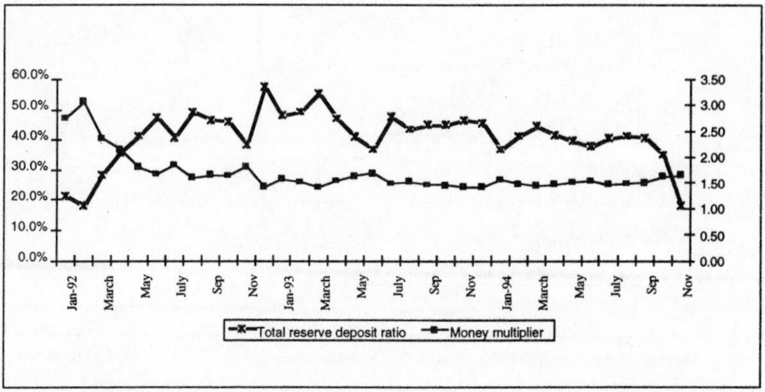

Source: Appendix 1, Tables A.2 and A.4.

A link can be demonstrated between the level of interest rates and liquidity in the economy which reinforces the view that monetary policy in 1992–3 was not tight.

As shown in Figure 3.13, the level of real interest rates reflects in part the availability of real balances and inflation expectations. In this figure, the interest rate shown is the interbank rate. Real interest rates were negative throughout 1992 and the first half of 1993, when credits were abundant. Assuming a lag of three months between the amount of real balances available in the economy and the interest rate (r at time $t + 3$), a strong correlation between the two can be observed: the more real money balances are available, the lower is the real interest rate charged three months later and vice versa.

Another reason to dismiss the credit squeeze argument is that foreign-exchange deposits of firms and households (Appendix 1, Table A.6) grew quite markedly during 1992. Even if these deposits were not evenly distributed, their magnitude suggests that quite a large proportion of firms held such deposits, evidently as a hedge against inflation and rouble depreciation.[7]

Figure 3.13. Real money balances and the real interest rate

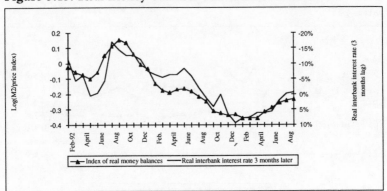

Sources: Quarterly Bulletin of the CBR and *Russian Economic Trends* (1993), Vol. 2, No. 3, and (1994), Vol. 3, No. 3.

3.3. Why was monetary policy relaxed?

The volume of inter-enterprise arrears (IEA) grew from R34 billion at the end of December 1991 to R3,004 billion at the end of June 1992[8] – that is, to 66% of GDP.[9] The industrial sector claimed that inter-enterprise arrears were the result of excessively tight monetary policy. Since, as we have seen, monetary policy was not tight, this claim cannot be taken seriously. The underlying cause had more to do with the lack of credibility of the government reform programme.

Nevertheless, while the main reason for the development of arrears was that firms were still behaving as they had under the old regime – that is, without the constraint of financial discipline – various industrial groups made their voices heard in parliament. Politically the problem took on such proportions that the government could no longer ignore the problem altogether. Unfortunately, the way it was tackled seriously endangered the macrostabilization process during 1992.

It is important to establish at the outset what is included in the definition of inter-enterprise arrears in Russia. The recorded stock of inter-enterprise arrears consisted of the aggregate amount of payment orders presented to the banking system, but not executed due to the insufficiency of funds in clients' accounts, and recorded in the so-called Kartoteka 2: the name of the file in which, in standard Soviet practice, the unpaid debts of an enterprise were

Figure 3.14. Inter-enterprise arrears as a percentage of Rbs M2 and bank credits

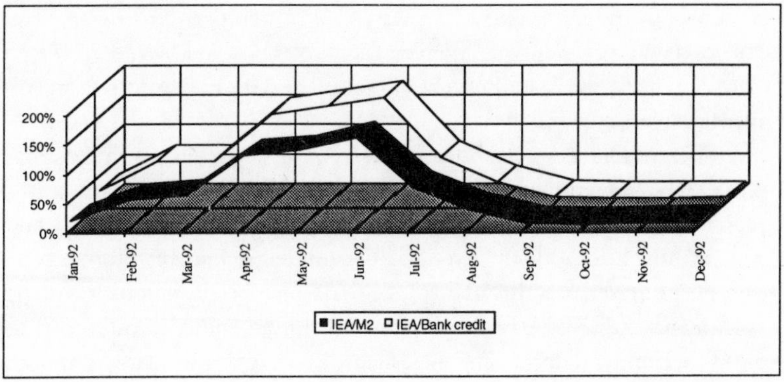

Source: Appendix 1, Table A.11.

accumulated by the enterprise's bank. As money came in, the bank was meant to pay the debts automatically in the order in which they had been incurred. Payment orders are taken to include tax arrears. On the basis of this definition, the scale of the problem was much exaggerated. Moreover, some of the 'arrears' amounted to voluntary trade credit extended by one enterprise to another as part of standard business practice.

The problem of arrears was not new. It had already emerged in 1987 (for a detailed study see Hansson, 1991a, p. 21). Firms were used to delivering products without having to press for payment, which had always been guaranteed by the state in accordance with the state orders laid down in the plan. The state enterprise sector was financed from both the government budget and the banking sector, which covered not only its capital requirements but also its losses (for more details see Ickes and Ryterman, 1992). This system officially ended on 1 July 1992 with a presidential decree for all inter-enterprise debt outstanding on that date. As a result of the closing of the Kartoteka 2,[10] inter-enterprise arrears decreased to 5% of GDP in September 1992 as compared to 66% in June 1992 (Figure 3.14, above, and Appendix 1, Table A.11).

Two solutions to the arrears problem were proposed. The first was embodied in the presidential decree of 1 July 1992, which provided for a two-stage approach. Inter-enterprise positions were to be reduced to net values by the end of August; then, net debtors would first be allowed a three-month period for reimbursement of outstanding debt. As the bankruptcy law was not operational (it came into effect on 1 March 1993), debtor enterprises that had not settled by that time would then be taken over by a specialized agency to be created inside the State Property Committee (GKI). This provision was never enforced.

A different solution was offered by the CBR and was the cause of a dispute between the government and Gerashchenko. The starting-point was a telegram to the regional branches of the CBR, signed by Gerashchenko and dated 28 July 1992, which permitted the mutual settlement of enterprise debts. He promised to write off up to R1.5 trillion owed by enterprises to the government, and to issue credits of up to R1 trillion to enable enterprises to pay off their mutual debts. The Gerashchenko telegram was largely at odds with the presidential decree, providing as it did for the netting and reimbursement phase to be followed by the creation of this special R1 trillion credit generally considered to be a bailing-out facility, with obvious dangers for inflation and financial stabilization. The telegram, moreover, contravened the agreement reached with the IMF, according to which credit grants should have been limited to R1,500 billion up to the end of 1992. Achievement of such targets was forecast to reduce inflation to 9% per month. However, in the face of political pressure from parliament and the various industrial lobbies, the government backed down and the CBR had its way: that is, inter-enterprise arrears were converted into money.

Special accounts called 725 accounts were created for each state enterprise, on which its inter-enterprise assets and liabilities were registered. 'The mechanism provided for a "one-time" payment claim between and only between state enterprises at 1 July 1992. The payment took the form of an accounting entry and concerned not only payments to state enterprises in Russia but also payments to state enterprises in the other republics of the CIS ... the 725 account was for claims to and from state enterprises located in Russia and the 721 accounts for claims to and from state-enterprises located in other enterprises of the CIS.' (Boissieu et al., 1993, p. 19) Enterprises with positive balances could then use their 'special accounts' to pay off their inter-enterprise arrears. State firms which received such payments could in turn use them to pay off their own inter-enterprise arrears. Initially it was decided that the netting out of inter-enterprise arrears would end on 5 October 1992; but the payment system was unable to cope with the volume of inter-enterprise arrears, and the deadline was therefore extended to November 1992. Boissieu et al. (1993, p. 24) note:

> Another important consequence of the netting system was essentially to worsen the loan portfolios of the banks who were the ones who ultimately ended up with the debit balances of companies who did not receive payment from suppliers. The banks became *de facto* suppliers of working capital finance to companies to whom in many cases they had refused to lend in the first place.

We have already seen that the credit crunch hypothesis – contrary to what Calvo and Kumar (1994, p. 326) assumed for former socialist countries – is not relevant as an explanation for the way in which inter-enterprise arrears developed in Russia. Rather, the soft budget constraint on firms encouraged the accumulation of inter-enterprise arrears and ultimately the monetization of these arrears by the CBR. Four other factors were also relevant.

The system of payments

Commercial banks handled the flow of inter-enterprise transactions, but most payments were routed through the CBR with its 1,400 regional cash-settlement centres (*Rashyotnye Kassovye Tsentry* – RKTs). This centralized clearing system was introduced in October 1991 and replaced the former system of direct bilateral clearing between bank offices (*Mezh-filialny oborot* – MFOs), which had been outgrown by the emergence of a large number of banks.[11] But this centralization forced all payments to flow through one single institution, the CBR, since direct links between commercial banks through correspondent accounts were not allowed until May 1992. This point, however, is not clear. It seems that from May 1992 banks were legally permitted to hold correspondent accounts only with banks from other republics. However, while officially all bank clearings within Russia were still required to go through the RKT system, certain groups of banks began creating their own clearing system, independent of the CBR, in order to speed up payments. The CBR seemed to tolerate such a system, but since few commercial banks had the means to do it they charged a huge fee for the transactions handled in their system (8% commission).

Payment orders were all executed on paper, and processing was manual. While the payer's account was debited only when the order entered the system at the payer's bank, the payee was not credited until the actual payment document was received by its bank. As a result payments could take between 14 and 17 days, or more, depending on the location, and a very large float was created which had a negative impact on the liquidity of enterprises.

The delays in the payment system partly explain why the commercial banks held such a large quantity of funds in their correspondent accounts at the Central Bank. This would have been unnecessary if a multilateral clearing system had been created allowing a bank (and all its branches) to have only one account at the Central Bank, and if banks could have opened correspondent accounts directly with other banks. It is certainly what they started doing in 1993 and 1994 (Cochrane and Ickes, 1994, p. 26).

Cash and non-cash

As noted in Chapter 1, the Russian monetary system was divided into cash and non-cash segments. The former consisted of the household, agricultural and small private business sectors, while the latter derived from the state enterprise sector. The two areas were linked together on the one side through wages and social security payments, and on the other side through retail sales (Ofer, 1992, p. 11). With price liberalization, enterprises marked up prices and increased profits, and the resulting increase in bank deposits – which could not be switched into cash money – was used to pay off arrears (World Bank, 1992, p. 19). But this effect was more than offset by other factors. Enterprise credit, already abundant in late 1991, was only moderately tightened: and the opportunity to obtain cheap credit (especially attractive with high inflation) removed any incentive for producers to sell their output to pay their suppliers, while at the same time the stockpiling of inventories was exacerbated by inflationary expectations, encouraging enterprises to forestall marketing.

The main stimulant of inter-enterprise arrears was in fact the combination of relatively easy credit in the non-cash enterprise sector with a cash squeeze in the household sector, in the form of limited issuing of banknotes.

In January 1992 the Russian government was some R19 billion behind in payment of wages, pensions and benefits, and by June 1992 these arrears had risen to R221.6 billion (Appendix 1, Table A.12). In other words, the cash shortage was itself reflected in a build-up of wage and other payment arrears by the government. The resulting fall in purchasing power, besides undermining the strategic reform objective of encouraging the production and distribution of consumer goods and services, had the immediate effect of depressing retail activity, which in January 1992 fell to 37% of its real level in January 1991 (World Bank, 1992, p. 19). The lack of retail sales created arrears, initially from sellers to suppliers, and thence through the whole economy.

The correct solution to the problem, therefore, was not a further loosening of credit to enterprises, which would only further increase inventories. The first step should have been to end the dichotomy in the banking system between the cash and the non-cash circuits with the banking sector unable to fill the most basic function of allowing the depositor to withdraw deposits in the form of cash (Lipton and Sachs, 1992, pp. 38–9). This would have meant increasing 'the amount of cash in circulation relative to the amount of bank credit' (World Bank, 1992, p. 19), but not the amount of central bank credits available to enterprises.

The tax avoidance assumption

At the beginning of the reform programme in 1992, the government instituted a new system of taxation comprising a value added tax (VAT) of 28% and a unified profit tax.[12] The commercial banks were responsible for collecting these taxes. In principle, with high inflation, taxes are simply reduced by 'delaying cóllection on receivables' (Ickes and Ryterman, 1992, p. 21),[13] or by using inter-enterprise arrears to avoid the commercial banking system altogether. And, 'if delays lower tax collection, and lower tax collection increases money creation, then inflation will result, which ratifies the expectation of inflation that starts the process' (Ickes and Ryterman, 1992, p. 24).

However, in Russia delays in tax collection were not the problem (at least in 1992), because, as we shall see in the next section, VAT and profit tax had to be paid *ex ante*. So the way to evade taxes was either not to pay at all or not to report activities, which partly explains the unreliability of the output statistics.

All the foregoing explanations have in common the lack of credibility of the reform programme. Without a bankruptcy law in place, and without a clear commitment by the government to exercise tight control over credit, this lack of credibility is not surprising. However, if the existence of a bankruptcy law is a necessary condition for imposing financial discipline on enterprises, the law in itself is not sufficient (Rostowski, 1993): experienced courts and liquidators are essential.[14] This was a key point overlooked by many Western economists contemplating the end of communism in the late 1980s.

Credibility of the stabilization programme

For how long can inter-enterprise arrears persist and banks provide new credits? The answer is straightforward. As long as the banks 'fear the financial impact on their balance sheets and governments fear the unemployment consequences' (Brainard, 1990, p. 15), firms will remain on a soft budget constraint. Indeed, 'After a few months, firms realise that they are not the only ones undergoing financial problems. They may start raising wages despite tight financial constraints in the expectation that the government will not let a large section of the productive system go bankrupt.' (Calvo and Coricelli, 1992, p. 208) In Poland, there was no inter-enterprise arrears explosion during the first year of transition; this reflected the credibility of the stabilization programme (Rostowski, 1993). For two years from 1990 to 1992, the Polish authorities chose to do nothing, with the result that at the end of this period the problem did not worsen; indeed, it almost completely disappeared (Rostowski, 1993, p. 21).

Avoiding renewed accumulation of inter-enterprise arrears will depend on the credibility of monetary discipline. If all the signals (e.g. interest rates) are the right ones the programme will hold, forcing firms to try to survive not by giving credits to each other but by genuinely attempting to adjust to the new surroundings.

We saw earlier that interest rates on credit and deposits, in real terms, were negative (Appendix 1, Table A.10) until the beginning of the third quarter of 1993. This differs from the situation in Poland and the former CSFR where, after six months of the stabilization programme, real interest rates were positive (Rostowski, 1993, p. 9).

Starting in 1993, inter-enterprise arrears ceased to be a dominant problem in both political and actual terms. One reason for this may be that with the cancellation of Kartoteka 2, no new system was put in place whereby the commercial banks could compile the information on unpaid claims and report them to the CBR. But despite the difficulty of establishing a full record because the whole system of registration of inter-enterprise arrears had been changed (see Boissieu et al., 1993, p. 24), it is clear that the most important reason was that most enterprises asked for prepayment, with the notable exception of those enterprises which relied on state orders – mainly the MIC and the energy and transport sectors. With the prepayment mechanism, firms became more genuinely subject to a hard budget constraint, and a real change of behaviour began to occur in Russian state enterprises (Boissieu et al., 1993;

Fan and Schaffer, 1994). In 1994, inter-enterprise arrears did not disappear but became increasingly confined to the energy sector, where they were used as a form of cheap credits, for instance to electricity suppliers, or by oil exporters to suppliers to finance capital exports. In 1994, too, the government contributed to the problem by delaying its expenditures when tax revenues fell short. So to say that in 1994 arrears were just 'bad debts' (Melitz and Waysand, 1994, p. 6) is not entirely true.

In any event, our discussion has shown that when the money supply was tightened the inflation rate decreased, even if other factors were also at work. In other words, despite more systemic problems like the monetary and payment system, Russia is in this respect no different from any other economy in transition nor in essence from Western capitalist countries.

The Russian government's mistakes were made in reaction to fears and pressures, notably the output slump – which allowed enterprises, especially in the MIC but also in the agricultural and energy sectors, to exert successful pressure to receive the financing necessary to pay their workers and obtain the inputs required for continued production of unsaleable goods[15] – and the threat of unemployment, especially in cities dependent on one or two factories. It was argued that catastrophe could only be averted by large-scale subsidies to such industries. Unemployment did indeed remain low, because the subsidized credits (part of which were assumed *ex post* to be grants) allowed enterprises to avoid employment restructuring: 'The dominant objective of Russian firms has generally been to restrain the rate of job separations ... One implication is that the current employment overhang is indeed very large.' (Commander, Liberman and Yemtsov, 1993, p. 2)

In 1992, one factor that might have helped the Gaidar government to resist all these inflationary pressures was financial support from the West. As Yeltsin (1994, p. 165) wrote with regard to April 1992, 'The mood in the government was one of concern, if not depression. The only reassuring note was the promise of the Group of Seven to rapidly provide major financial aid.' The role of foreign aid in promoting the resolution of the Russians is the subject of the next chapter.

4 THE IMPORTANCE OF EXTERNAL FINANCING

Early in 1992, the reformist government led by Yegor Gaidar was promised a Western aid package of US$24 billion, and designed the reform programme accordingly. The aid was supposed to come in the second half of 1992 to support the budget and stabilization. After four months of radical reform, the government was hard-pressed to survive a hostile backlash at the Congress of People's Deputies in April 1992. Gaidar struggled on in an increasingly adverse political climate for a further seven months. In that period, none of the promised assistance – an IMF standby arrangement (SBA), a $6 billion exchange stabilization fund, an official debt rescheduling deal – materialized, with the exception of an interim IMF credit of $1 billion disbursed in August 1992 for reserves purpose only. In 1992 the World Bank approved US$670 million; this was not disbursed until the end of 1993. The brief opportunity for major external support for reform at its height was lost.

During the Congress of December 1992, Gaidar was replaced as Prime Minister by Victor Chernomyrdin. The slowdown (or worse) in the momentum of reform, first visible in April, was now unmistakable.

4.1. The measured budget deficit

There are two ways to look at the measured budget deficit: the cash deficit of the enlarged government sector and the cash deficit of the consolidated state budget. Looking at the cash definition of the consolidated budget, Professor Jeffrey Sachs, a leading foreign adviser to the Russian government, argued that stabilization was within reach in 1992. Sachs, critic of Western hesitation, published numerous articles in the press and elsewhere (Sachs, 1994b, 1994c) explaining why financial aid, if it had been delivered in 1992 as promised, would have helped Russia to stabilize. This view was not shared, however, in the IMF declarations at the time, which maintained that Russia was far from fiscal balance in the first half of 1992. As Sachs (1994b, p. 25) points out: 'The most important difference was that the IMF was counting as part of an "enlarged deficit" concept a portion of the imports financed by Western bilateral export credits.'

The cash deficit of the enlarged government sector
This includes the federal and local governments, the major extra-budgetary funds and unbudgeted import subsidies. Import subsidies (abolished only in 1994) were a source of the conflict; they were financed externally by tied credits – that is, Western bilateral export credits – and as such were not inflationary in the short term. The extra-budgetary funds were usually in surplus and so not really relevant from the standpoint of inflationary financing. The reason why the IMF included import subsidies in their calculation is that these revenues were claims on future revenues.[1]

Import subsidies were financed externally by tied credits from foreign governments, so that they did not have a direct impact on inflation. This explains the relatively low domestic CBR financing compared with the size of the budget deficit if import subsidies are included (Tables 4.1 and 4.2).

The basic mechanism of import subsidy (Sachs, 1994b, p. 25) was as follows. The lending export agency makes available a line of credit to purchase goods in the earmarked country. The Russian Foreign Trade Organization (FTO) takes possession of the goods at a price lower than the actual price paid by the Russian government. The FTO then sells the goods and retains the rouble earnings. The export credit in turn is owed by the Russian government.

Import subsidies were the most important remaining price control and applied to centralized imports. The subsidies reflected the difference between the controlled domestic price and world price of the imports and were intended to insulate domestic consumers of imports from world prices. These imported goods – mainly grains – were provided to economic agents at prices below the price implied by the market exchange rate. Following the unification of the exchange rate in July 1992, this was equivalent to a subsidy. Indeed, the multiple exchange-rate system applied to centralized imports until August 1992 was replaced by explicit budgetary subsidies. On 21 August 1992 the Pricing Committee of the Russian Ministry of Economics and the Ministry of Finance established procedures for calculating the cost of imported foodstuffs, children's goods and certain types of raw materials and

Table 4.1. Summary of fiscal indicators (% of GDP)

	1991	1992	1993	1994 (preliminary)
1. Enlarged government balance[a]	−16.5	−20.5	−8.5	−10
2. Consolidated state balance		−11.1	−6.7	
of which				
federal government balance		−12.5	−7.3	−10.4
local government balance[b]		1.3	0.6	
3. Extra-budgetary funds balance[b]		2.5	0.6	
4. Unbudgeted federal import subsidies		11.9	2.3	0
5. Statistical discrepancy and float		−1.7	−0.6	
6. Total financing[c]		−18.8	−7.9	
(Enlarged government balance, adjusted)				
Nominal GDP (in trn of Rbs)		18.1	162.3	630

[a] Enlarged government deficit (2+3-4) defined as federal and local governments, plus extra-budgetary funds, plus unbudgeted import subsidies; average of quarterly ratios to GDP. For 1991, annual budget deficit (concept defined in IMF, 1992a) over annual GDP. Data based on information from the Ministry of Finance, i.e. not taking into account float and statistical discrepancy.

[b] Unconsolidated revenues and expenditures (inclusive of transfers).

[c] Based on domestic and foreign financing information, calculated here as (1-5).

Source: IMF (1995), Table 23, p. 84 .

Table 4.2. Financing of the enlarged government (% of GDP)

	1992	1993	1994: QII
Total financing	18.8	8	10
1. Domestic financing	6.7	5.5	9.7
Domestic bank financing	5.6	5	9.6
Monetary authorities	—	6.2	8.6
2. Foreign financing (i+ii)	12.1	2.6	0.2
i Foreign disbursements	12.7	2.7	0.9
Tied credits	11.6	2.7	0.7
Untied credits	0.6	0.4	0.15
ii Principal payments, cash	−1.1	−0.2	−0.6
Nominal GDP (Rtrn)	18.1	162.3	128.4

Source: IMF (1995), Table 27, p. 88.

equipment to be sold on the internal market. The procedures were based on special coefficients to be applied to the market exchange rate. For instance, from 1 November 1992 a coefficient of 0.3 was used for converting the cost of grain purchases. As a result, Canadian wheat was approximately as expensive to the Russian consumer as Russian wheat.

The cash deficit of the consolidated state budget
This comprised federal and local governments only. The cash budget deficit of the consolidated government was 11.1% in 1992, while the enlarged government deficit balance was 18.8% taking into account import subsidies and statistical discrepancy (Table 4.1).

4.2. Financing of the budget deficit

The following equation (Sachs, 1994b, c):

$$(4.1) \qquad \Delta P/P = \Delta M/M$$

means that the monthly price equation (π) equals the monthly rate of growth of money creation (θ) assuming a steady state (that is, $\pi = \theta + n$ with $n = 0$).

$$(4.2) \qquad D = d(Y)$$

where D equals the budget deficit, Y is the level of GDP and d is the ratio of the deficit to the GDP. As we saw above, this ratio must include quasi-fiscal expenditures, that is, central credits to enterprises financed via commercial banks (section 4.4).

There are three ways to finance the budget deficit – money creation, bonds and external financing:

$$(4.3) \qquad D = \Delta M + \Delta F + \Delta B$$

where ΔM is the change in money creation, ΔF is the change in foreign debt and ΔB is the change in domestic debt.

Combining these three equations and the definitions for d, f, and b which are the respective ratios as a percentage of GDP, the equation for inflation becomes the following:

(4.4) $\Delta P/P = (d-f-b)V$

V being defined as $V = GDP/M$. This states that the higher the income velocity of money, the higher the inflation.

Thus, assuming for instance a budget deficit ratio of 14.5% (i.e. total financing need was about 7.9% plus 6.8% of Central Bank credits to enterprises in 1993), no foreign financing, 0.1% of GDP of bond financing and a monthly velocity of about 1.2 for 1993, equation (4.4) gives a prediction for monthly inflation of $(14.7-0.0-0.1)(1.2) = 17.52\%$, that is, an annual inflation rate of 594%. It can easily be seen that, according to equation (4.4) the monthly inflation rate could have been lowered through the provision of external financing.

Table 4.3 looks in more detail at the financing of the enlarged budget deficit. We will subsequently analyse the three ways by which the deficit was financed.

Monetary financing
Table 4.3 shows that the monetary financing of the measured budget deficit in 1992 was about 5.5% while it decreased to 5% in 1993 and increased to about 10% in the second quarter of 1994 (due partly to the integration of the quasi-fiscal expenditures in the measured budget). The money-financed deficit was mainly financed by the variation of the monetary base; credits from commercial banks to local governments, for instance, were not allowed until May 1993. Table 4.3 shows that credits from commercial banks started to be positive only in the second quarter of 1994.

Financing government spending through the creation of base money is an alternative to explicit taxation. How much revenue in real terms the government can obtain from the printing of money depends on the size of the real money base as a percentage of GDP. The simplest measures of seigniorage are presented in Appendix 1, Table A.7:

First, the monthly change in the amount of rouble currency as a percentage of monthly GDP:

(4.5) $\Delta C/GDP = (C_{t}-C_{t-1})/\text{nominal monthly GDP} = SEC$

Second, the monthly change in the monetary base (defined in a broad sense, i.e. including excess reserves) as a percentage of monthly GDP:

Table 4.3. Financing of the enlarged deficit (in % of GDP)

	1992	1993	Q1 1994	Q2 1994
Total financing (1+2)	18.78	8.01	5.75	10.28
(Cumulative flows)				14.72
1. Domestic financing (i+ii)	6.63	5.42	5.34	9.97
i. Domestic bank financing	5.52	5.05	5.14	9.89
Monetary authorities net credit				
to government		6.16	6.25	8.80
Net credit from CBR	9.39	5.42	5.75	8.26
Rouble counterpart of government				
foreign exchange		0.74	0.50	0.62
Net credit from rest of banking system		−1.11	−1.11	1.01
Net credit from banks		−1.23		
Securities held by banks		0.12		
ii. Domestic non-bank financing	1.10	0.43	0.10	0.16
Principal repayment		−0.25		
Proceeds from privatization	0.55	0.18	0.10	0.16
Net proceeds form gold sales	1.10	0.49		
Securities held by the non bank sector				
2. Foreign financing (i+ii)	12.15	2.59	0.40	0.23
i. Foreign disbursements	12.71	2.77	0.91	0.86
ii. Principal payment, cash	−1.10	−0.18	−0.50	−0.62
Exchange rate, average period	222	933	1577	1877
Nominal GDP (Rtrn)	18.1	162.3	99.2	128.4

Source: IMF (1995) calculated from Table 27, p. 88.

$$(4.6)\ \Delta MB1/GDP = (MB1_t - MB1_{t-1})/\text{monthly nominal GDP} = SE1$$

Third, the monthly change in the monetary base defined in a narrow sense (without excess reserves) as a percentage of monthly GDP:

$$(4.7)\ \Delta MB2/GDP = (MB2_t - MB2_{t-1})/\text{monthly nominal GDP} = SE2$$

The definition of seigniorage adopted here is the flow definition, i.e. it corresponds to the amount of goods and services that the government can buy by issuing additional money or forcing commercial banks to hold more reserves. In Russia, as was noted earlier, the substantial holding of excess reserves resulted in even more tax for the government than expected – a real gift from commercial banks to the government. If we look at Table A.7 (Appendix 1), and calculate the respective monthly averages for 1992, 1993 and 1994, we find 20.5% for the calculation of seigniorage as a percentage of GDP with the monetary base inclusive of excess reserves and 10.6% otherwise; in 1993 the respective percentages were 11.5% and 8.5% while in 1994 seigniorage decreased sharply to 5.7% and 5.3%.[2]

The rapid decline of inflation tax receipts as measured by seigniorage is easily explained by the rising share of foreign deposits in M2 and by the improvement of settlements systems (especially with regard to excess reserves). This trend is damaging in the sense that if the government were to maintain a constant level of monetary financing of the budget, this would involve considerably more inflation. In other words, the fact that inflation is a tax means that if the tax base is shrinking as a result of economic agents converting their rouble assets into foreign currency assets, the tax itself has to increase in order to keep the same level of monetary financing. The alternatives, of course, are to reduce the budget deficit or to develop other forms of financing such as bond issues or foreign loans.

In Russia, base money (defined as currency outside the CBR plus required reserves plus commercial banks' correspondent accounts at the CBR – what we called excess reserves) over annualized GDP fell from 9% in December 1992 to 7% in December 1993 and 6% in November 1994. As emphasized by Koen and Marrese (1995, p. 9), the budget deficit, although large, was not dramatic (the enlarged deficit was 8.5% in 1993 while the consolidated state budget was about 7% – less than the Italian budget deficit during the same year). Italy's budget deficit in 1993 was 10.3% of GDP and about the same in 1992. However, the risk of high inflation was much greater because in Italy the ratio of base money to annual GDP was 15%, for instance, while in Russia, as mentioned earlier, it was 9% at the end of 1992 and 7% at the end of 1993. The absence of a domestic bond market at least in 1992 (see below), and in 1993–4 'the embryonic nature of the long term government securities market imply that a fiscal deficit/GDP ratio that may not be perceived as an immediate inflationary threat to industrialised countries could propel the Russian economy into hyperinflation' (Koen and Marrese, 1995, p. 9). This point reinforced the Sachs position because with a bond market in an infant stage and with no foreign financing forthcoming, the Russian government was left with the following choice: reducing the budget deficit either through higher revenues or lower expenditures; or financing it through credits from the Central Bank – that is, facing more inflation.

Bond financing
The three-month government securities started to be issued in May 1993, with a six-month issue in December 1993 and the one-year issue in October 1994 as an alternative to printing money to finance the budget deficit. This raised 0.1% GDP of revenue in 1993 and 0.5% in 1994, or 1.5% and 10% of the budget deficit respectively. The securities are mainly held by commercial banks.

In Chapter 5, we will see the relationship between the T-bill market, the foreign exchange and the inter-bank credit market; also that at the beginning of 1995, owing to high inflation, the yields on T-bills were very high and that the issue of bonds was hardly sufficient to repay the previous ones. In February 1995, as discussion on the SBA and inflation expectations decreased, so also did the yields, allowing the government to make credible projections for financing 40% of its deficit by new T-bill issues. The 1995 budget envisages R32 trn of T-bill sales to cover more than 40% of a projected R73 trn deficit.

Bond financing has many advantages over money financing – large budget deficits result in increased yields on T-bills rather than faster rates of monetary expansion, and their effect, if trusted, on interest rates and exchange rate. But in a context of high inflation, there are also dangers, since T-bills carry a market-determined interest rate and thus raise the future debt service.

External financing
Table 4.5 shows the official financial assistance actually delivered to Russia as compared with the aid promised.

For the IMF, the budget had to fit certain targets which are universal, the argument being that any budget deficit is inflationary however it is financed because debt has to be serviced in the future (Sargent and Wallace, 1981). Import subsidies were loans, so they increased the external debt and indirectly fed inflation by increasing the 'foreign expenditures' line. However, to withhold external financing on this basis was tough in the Russian case. Russia's debt service represented about 25% of GDP in 1992, the market for domestic government debt was non-existent and the economic potential enormous. The IMF later acknowledged its short-sightedness by creating a new 'Systemic Transformation Facility' (STF), offering reduced credits with higher conditionality. But this was in 1993, and even then the IMF did not

Table 4.5. Official financial assistance to Russia, 1992–3 (US$ bn)

	1992		1993		1992–3	
	A	D	A	D	A	D
IMF	9	1	13	1.5	22	2.5
World Bank	1.5	0	5	0.5	6.5	0.5
EBRD						
Bilateral[a]	13.5	14	10	6	23.5	20
Total	24	15	28	8	52	23
Memo items						
Aid from international agencies	10.5	1	18	2	28.5	3
Budgetary support[b]		0		2		2

A - Announced.

D - Delivered.

[a] Includes $2.5 billion of promised relief on interest payments that was not formally granted in 1992.

[b] Estimates of aid that was directly in support of budget financing, not counting debt rescheduling. In 1993, approximately $2.5 billion could be used for budgetary support: $1 billion of the IMF loan, $0.5 billion of the World Bank loan and approximately $0.5 billion of Western support.

Source: IMF, press release, 1 February 1994, quoted in Sachs (1994c), p. 4.

lend the bulk of what it had ostensibly promised. The key agreement was not signed until March 1995.

The alternative, Sachs, approach (1994b, 1994c), by concentrating on the actual monetary needs of the budget deficit and by emphasizing the necessity and timing of financial aid by the West, allows a country in transition a relatively large budget deficit by IMF standards together with a relatively low inflation rate. This provides the possibility, in a first phase, of transferring to the budget social spending previously managed by enterprises (themselves directly financed by the CBR). Such expenditure would be subject to normal parliamentary pressure rather than industrial lobbies.

4.3. Increasing revenues and reducing expenditures

In a context of high inflation, increasing tax revenues is not an easy task. Moreover, the fiscal system of an economy in transition is usually in severe need of reforms, and this takes time – which further strengthens the case for strong front-loaded external financing with the greatest political momentum behind reform.

In the Russian case, the fiscal system was complicated, opaque and inefficient, making it virtually impossible to increase revenues, at least in the short term. In fact, during the period 1992–4, revenues as a percentage of GDP decreased, shifting the burden of reducing the budget deficit on to expenditure cuts.

In the literature the benefits of inflationary finance are balanced by the costs for explicit fiscal revenues (Mourmouras and Tijerina, 1994). The so-called Tanzi effect did not apply, at least during 1992 and part of 1993, because taxes had to be paid in advance and also in view of a tacit deal between enterprises and the government to the effect that: 'You pay your taxes and we give you directed credits.' At the end of 1993 and in 1994, however, as directed credits were phased out (section 4.4), and the structure of the economy changed (with more privatized firms coming into existence), collecting taxes became difficult and revenues as a percentage of GDP decreased quite substantially. This was consistent with the idea introduced by Tanzi (1978) that inflationary finance weakens public finances if high rates of inflation combined with significant collection lags erode the real value of explicit revenues.

Revenues
Tax revenues in Russia fell from 29% of GDP in 1992 to 27% in 1994 (Table 4.6). In 1994, profit taxes and VAT were substantially below the level of 1993 despite an increase in profit taxes from 32% to 38% and a 3% VAT increase (from 20% and 10% respectively to 23% and 13% respectively) earmarked for subsidization of the coal and agricultural sectors. Most revenues came from excise and from foreign economic activities (i.e. export industries' profits plus export and import tariffs). The fall in tax revenues was due to poor compliance,[3] statistical distortions and numerous tax exemptions.[4]

In January 1992 VAT on consumer purchases was introduced at 28%, replacing a 5% sales tax and the turnover tax. On 16 July 1992 parliament decided to reduce the VAT rate to 15% for selected items, mainly food (such as pasta, flour, dairy products, vegetable oil and children's goods), and to leave the current 28% rate unchanged until the end of 1992 for other goods. From 1 January 1993 the general rate was reduced to 20% and the rate for selected goods to 10%, which contributed substantially to the decline in the ratio of VAT to GDP from 11.1% in 1992 to 6.9% in 1993 (Table 4.6).

Table 4.6. Consolidated revenues as % of GDP, 1992–4

	1992	1993	1994
GDP (Rtrn)	18.064	162.3	630.00
Revenue (as a percentage of GDP)	29.00	28.50	27.00
of which:			
Personal income tax	2.40	2.70	2.70
Profit tax	8.70	10.30	7.80
VAT	11.10	6.90	5.80

Sources: IMF (1995), Table 25, p. 86; and *Current Statistical Survey*, Goskomstat of Russia, January 1995, monthly magazine (in English), p. 55.

Receipts from VAT as a share of overall government revenue rose from about 27% in the first quarter of 1992 to nearly 40% in the fourth quarter (Table 4.7). VAT became the largest single source of revenue during the second quarter of 1992. As a percentage of GDP its proceeds rose from 5.5% in Q1 to 14.8% in Q4. This partly reflected the netting-out and new injection of credits to settle inter-enterprise arrears, since VAT was also due on past payments.

In the case of VAT and the profit tax, payments were paid in advance from the middle of 1992, and collected twice a month. *Russian Economic Trends* (1993, vol. 2, no. 1, p. 10) notes:

> Most VAT payments have to be paid in advance (i.e. before the actual tax liability accrues). In particular, state enterprises must pay VAT twice a month equal to their expected tax liability over the following two weeks. These advance payments are reconciled with actual tax liabilities once per quarter; firms which have underpaid must pay interest on the tax arrears, but firms which are owed money by the government receive no interest compensation. In addition, since 16 July 1992 the government has delayed VAT refunds due for purchasers of inputs until after the input is actually used in the production process. The pre-payment system implies that higher expected inflation boosts the real revenue received by the government – the tax liability is commensurate to the price level expected over the tax period, and with a higher rate of expected inflation, the government receives more taxes before the higher rate of inflation materialises.

Table 4.7. Summary of quarterly consolidated revenue in 1992, as % of GDP

	Q1	Q2	Q3	Q4	1992
GDP (Rbn, current prices)	1,831.9	2,733.0	5,042.2	8,457.4	18,064.5
Revenue (as % of GDP)	19.4	24.4	24.7	35.0	29.0
VAT	5.5	6.9	9.1	14.8	11.1
Tax on oil and gas	0	0	0	1	0.5
Profit tax	5.6	10.8	7.8	9.2	8.7
Household income	1.8	2.2	2.2	2.7	2.4
Export taxes	1.1	1	1.3	2.4	1.7
Import tariff[a]			0.7	0.1	0.3

[a] From 1 September 1992 import tariffs were increased from 5% to 15%.
Source: Calculated from IMF (1993a, Tables 13 and 14); Goskomstat.

The practice of bi-monthly collection avoided the problem of the erosion of the real value of taxation owing to inflation during the delays in tax collection (the Tanzi or Oliveira–Tanzi effect).

Thereafter, however, VAT revenues fell substantially, from 11.1% of GDP in 1992 to 6.9% in 1993 and 5.8% in 1994. One of the reasons for the 1993 fall was that 'the Supreme Soviet exempted imported goods from VAT if contracts had been signed before the start of the year. This exemption sparked a massive campaign to re-write contracts, with the result that the VAT only raised Rbs 400 bn (0.25% GDP) from imports.' (Nagel, 1994, p. 2)

The second biggest source of revenue for the budget was profit tax. Yield from this increased from 8.7% of GDP in 1992 to 10.3% of GDP in 1993 (Table 4.6). It was collected three times per month from state and private enterprises on *ex ante* profits and once per quarter on *ex post* profits from small enterprises (i.e. those with fewer than 200 employees for industry, fewer than 100 for services and fewer than 50 for retail trade). One reason why it was such an important source of revenue was that profits and wages were linked: wages above four times the minimum wage (in 1993 this was changed to six times)[5] could not be deducted from cost in the calculation of profits and were taxed as profits at the rate of 32%.[6] By the fourth quarter of 1992 the profit tax was an especially important source of revenue since the minimum wage remained at R900 per month, while the average wage rose from R7,379 in September to R16,071 in December 1992.

In 1994, however, the profit tax fell from 10.3% of GDP to 7.8% (January–October 1994). This was due to a combination of measures like profit tax exemptions and a change in the calculation of the excess wage tax. 'An increase in the wage norm deductible as costs under the profit tax, from 4 to 6 times the minimum wage. When combined with the simultaneous increase in the minimum wage of 90%, this change is estimated to imply a reduction in the average burden of the profit tax of about 20 percent.' (IMF, 1995, p. 16) The explanation lies mainly in tax evasion and firms not reporting their activities.

Expenditures

Statistical problems in the measurement of expenditures are endless. The classification of the IMF (1995) is chosen here. In 1993 and 1994 substantial expenditure cuts were made, notably in the federal budget.

In 1992, the largest item of spending for the year as a whole was 'subsidies' (Table 4.8), which included import subsidies associated with centralized imports (mainly reflecting the highly depreciated rouble) but not unbudgeted subsidies. These amounted to 14.2% of GDP. It also included non-import subsidies divided between producers and consumers. Producer subsidies went mainly to the coal, agriculture and defence sectors. Subsidies to agriculture were high in 1992 and 1993 but as the IMF (1995) emphasized, the comparison is made difficult because some directed credits were passed in the budget in 1993.[7] Producer subsidies took various forms, such as interest-rate subsidies channelled through commercial banks. Consumer subsidies covered heating, food, rent and transport, and were mainly provided by local governments. Melitz and Waysand (1994, p. 24) estimated that industry and households paid on average about 15% of world prices for energy in 1992 and 30% of these prices in 1993. Subsidies in 1993 decreased sharply as centralized imports were phased out.

In 1993 external debt service increased from 0.9% in 1992 to 1.6%. The external debt of Russia (or former Soviet Union) amounted to about $84 bn at the end of 1993, of which $70 bn was owed to the West. This compared with $78.7 bn in 1992. In 1992, Russia repaid only $2.5–3 bn out of almost $10 bn due. It sought a deferral of the main part of its foreign debt repayment for a long period – 10–15 years.

Table 4.8. State budget, economic classification of expenditures (in % of GDP)[a]

	1992 in % of GDP	1993 in % of GDP	1994 (April–May), preliminary
Total expenditures	38.4	35.2	36.1
Wage bill[b]	4.8	8.1	
Subsidies[c]	14.2	7.3	
Defence[d]	4.7	4.4	4.2
External debt service, cash basis	0.9	1.6	
Operation and maintenance	6.9	4	
Investment[e]	2.7	5	
Unbudgeted import subsidies	11.9	2.3	
Nominal GDP (Rbn)	18064	16230!	

[a] Based on IMF estimates. Excludes extra-budgetary funds.

[b] Includes social security contributions, but excludes defence-sector wages.

[c] Includes only import subsidies associated with centralized imports in the budget, but not unbudgeted import subsidies associated with tied foreign credits.

[d] Excludes subsidies for conversion, which are classified under subsidies, but includes defence-sector wages

[e] Excludes investment in defence sector.

Source: IMF, 1995, Table 28, p. 89.

4.4. Directed credits or quasi-fiscal expenditures

So-called 'directed credits' were used for two purposes: to provide liquidity to the banking system; and to support specific enterprises, sectors and regions in Russia and in the FSRs. These credits were allocated according to political bargaining rather than market considerations. Because state enterprises undertook a large proportion of social expenditure (housing, kindergartens, medical care, etc.) and unemployment insurance (Boycko and Shleifer, 1994), this gave them the necessary negotiating power to obtain credits at subsidized interest rates. Since these credits were directly funded by the CBR, they did not appear in the budget; and they were also highly inflationary. Both the budget deficit and the directed credit programmes were financed (at least in 1992) by money creation. The confusion of fiscal and monetary policy made the system of funds transfer to enterprises complex and non-transparent (World Bank and IMF, 1993; Freinkman, 1994).

One of the justifications offered for these directed credits was to keep the level of employment stable; but, as pointed out by various authors (e.g. Easterly and Vieira da Cunha, 1993; Sachs, 1993), it would have been cheaper to have financed direct provision of welfare benefits to workers. And in order to promote faster change in the commercial banking system, it would have been highly beneficial to move to a straight discount window. Credit auctions were not introduced until February 1994 and even then represented only a small share of refinancing to banks.

Directed credits were allocated following requests from enterprises to the Supreme Soviet, the government and even in some cases directly to the CBR alone: 'The CBR itself initiated special subsidised directed credit programs in 1992 (about 30% of total CBR directed credits), which were targeted at expanding working capital of enterprises and reducing the burden of the arrears crisis.' (Freinkman, 1994, p. 7) The commercial banks were left as little more than the passive instruments of such decisions – reminiscent of their position under the old command-administrative system – and the credits were rarely reimbursed.[8]

In early 1993, in order to slow down the allocation of credits, a Commission for Credit Policy (CPC) was reactivated. The Commission, which includes representatives of the Ministries of Finance, Economy and Agriulture as well as the CBR (see IMF, 1993a, p. 25), was put in charge of controlling directed credits. It was supposed to be the sole authority empowered to decide whether a credit should be granted: its decision in any given case was conveyed directly to the ministry concerned, which in turn informed the Ministry of Finance, which itself notified the CBR. The CBR then instructed its regional branches to designate the commercial banks through which the credit should be chanelled.

Table 4.9 shows the breakdown of total CBR credits for 1992 and 1993: in 1992 6.6% of GDP went to the budget, 20% to enterprises and a substantial figure of 5% to other former Soviet republics;[9] in 1993, the figures were, respectively, 6.9%, 6.8% and 1.5%. The table shows that Central Bank credits to enterprises fell into two categories. The first kind were channelled through commercial banks, and amounted to R2,804 billion or 15.5% of GDP in 1992 and R8,150 billion or 5% in 1993. These were directed or 'centralized' credits in the sense that the Central Bank informed the commercial banks (usually former state banks specializing in the sector chosen for the credit) through its regional branches which state

Table 4.9. Breakdown of total CBR credits and share in GDP, 1992–3 (Rbn)

	1992 in Rbn	% ratio to 1992 GDP	1993 in Rbn	% ratio to 1993 GDP
Total CBR credits[a]	5703	31.6%	24790	15.3%
Total GDP (yearly) in Rbn	18064		162301	
Budget	1189	6.6%	11276	6.9%
Enterprises of which:	3608	20.0%	11111	6.8%
via commercial banks	2804	15.5%	8150	5.0%
Agriculture and Roskleboprodukt	1300	7.2%	3616	2.2%
Energy	400	2.2%	193	0.1%
Northern Territories	300	1.7%	2134	1.3%
Industry	500	2.8%	466	0.3%
Other	304	1.7%	421	0.3%
Regions with urgent needs			1320	0.8%
via Ministry of Finance	804	4.5%	2961	1.8%
Working capital	600	3.3%		
Investment	105	0.6%	700	0.4%
Military conversion[b]	77	0.4%		
Roskhleboprodukt	22	0.1%	1566	1.0%
Other budget loans			695	0.4%
Other republics	906	5.0%	2403	1.5%

[a] The percentage of CBR-directed credit/CBR stock gross credit to banks amounted to 99% in 1992 and in 1993.
[b] In 1993, conversion credits for military-industrial enterprises classified as subsidies in fiscal accounts.
Source: Calculated from CBR data, Ministry of Finance, and IMF (1995), Table 35, p. 96.

enterprises should receive the credit and at what interest rate. These credits were concentrated on the agriculture and energy sectors,[10] and most of them were designed to compensate for the price controls which stayed in force in those sectors. For instance, in bread production any producer price above R12/kg was subsidized. The sizeable energy subsidy represented, broadly speaking, the difference between domestic prices of primary energy sources and the value of potential energy exports, restricted through quotas (World Bank and IMF, 1993, p. 7).

The second type of Central Bank-directed credits to enterprises was those delivered via the Ministry of Finance. These amounted to R804 billion in 1992 (4.5% of GDP) and R2,961 billion or 1.8% of GDP in 1993 (Table 4.9). Such credits were allocated off-budget to enterprises. They enabled the Ministry of Finance to borrow a greater amount from the CBR than the ceiling imposed by the Supreme Soviet, since special credit lines had been secured for these operations separate from the overall credit ceiling (IMF, 1993a, p. 15). These credits included military conversion subsidies and working capital credits.

Subsidies to the military-industrial complex (MIC) were used to maintain employment in a sector that would otherwise have been left crippled by the collapse of state defence procurement orders. Some R77 billion were allocated to such subsidies during 1992. By 1993 civilian products accounted for nearly 80% of MIC enterprises, rising from around 44% in 1988 (Gavrilenkov and Koen, 1994, p. 11). The origin of working capital credits lay in the central planning system, when enterprises automatically obtained working capital from the budget (Cochrane and Ickes, 1994, p. 20). During the second half of 1992 the government faced an increasing number of complaints from firms claiming that they could not borrow from commercial banks, because the interest rate was too high (it was in fact negative in real terms) and the term too short (usually three months or less). The government agreed to extend working capital loans through the Central Bank, usually for two years at subsidized interest rates.[11] The sum allocated – R600 billion – was meant to restore the 1992 real value of working capital (Sachs, 1993, p. 3).

By the end of 1992, credits to state enterprises allocated either by the central bank or by the government amounted to almost 20% of GDP; another 25% of GDP was allocated in explicit subsidies through the budget (Table 4.10). Thus a total of 45% of GDP was devoted to financial transfers to state enterprises for 1992 alone. The numerous subsidies combined with the directed credit to enterprises amounted to an impressive transfer to enterprise in 1992. In 1993 and 1994, directed credits programmes were decreased, mostly in the areas of social expenditures and unemployment insurance.

The problem with these credits was not confined to their size. They were, in addition, allocated largely at concessional interest rates substantially below the refinance rate (which was itself negative in real terms), the difference

Table 4.10. Explicit subsidies to state enterprises in 1992

	Value (Rbn)	% GDP
	4454	24.7
Agriculture	308	1.7
Coal	180	1
Local budgets	585	3.2
Other	30	0.2
Interest rates	630	3.5
CBR credits	495	2.7
Government credits	135	0.7
Centralized imports	2721	15.1

Sources: IMF (1993a), Table A1, p. 139; Goskomstat.

being paid by the federal budget.[12] As such these credits placed a heavy burden on the government's finances. For instance, at the beginning of 1993 agricultural credits were allocated at an annual rate of 25% (plus 3% commission for the commercial bank), while the annual refinance rate stood at 100% (30 March 1993, Appendix 1, Table A.3): the 75% difference was covered by the subsidy supplied by the federal budget at the end of the fiscal year. Total subsidies on interest rates, in respect of both CBR and government credits, amounted to 3.5% of GDP in 1992 (Table 4.10).

Theoretically, the responsibility for these credits and their repayment lay with the commercial banks, which acted as intermediaries for the funds. The credits were provided for one year (while commercial credits were granted on average for no more than three months), and firms had a strong incentive to repay them in order to get more funds. Because real interest rates were negative, directed credits amounted effectively to grants, and at least until the end of 1994 no action was taken against a bank or a firm which could not reimburse such a loan. Banks for their part showed no reluctance to accept such credits, especially because they did not usually channel the money to the earmarked firm immediately. However, on 1 October 1993 subsidized credits were cancelled, and in November 1993 interest rates started to be positive. With the risk of non-repayment increasing, banks began to refuse to channel these CBR credits.

The debate between Sachs and the IMF illustrates the importance of the relationship between economic and political stabilization for contemporary economists concerned with the problems of economic reform in post-Soviet

Russia. Economic liberalization is assumed to go hand in hand with political democratization; and, for a time, it did indeed appear that the two were mutually reinforcing and accelerating. However, if the adjustment has to be financed exclusively by reducing expenditures (while the financial market is in its infancy), political stability may be jeopardized. The point is reinforced by the nature of an economy in transition, where for a time the budget deficit has to be, if not increased, at least constant while the government restructures its expenditures, so as to take over all the quasi-fiscal items from the Central Bank. Rapid inflation could undermine the present Russian government, leading to a popular reaction not only against market reforms but also against democratic politics. A clear warning was given by the parliamentary election results of December 1993, which led to the resignation of key reformers, notably Boris Fyodorov and Yegor Gaidar. This fear encouraged the government to tighten its monetary stance somewhat in the course of 1994, leading to some stabilization of the inflation rate. But, as shown by the October 1994 rouble crash and its consequences, the danger that inflation could accelerate again remains real. If the only way for Russia to control the inflation rate is to decrease or sequestrate expenditures, the resulting hardship and social tension could have equally, if not more, deleterious effects. The perceived risks of 'tight' economic policies – as well as their prospective benefits – should be recognized to be of profound importance by Western governments and international organizations, notably the International Monetary Fund, as they seek to formulate their policies towards Russia.

5 FINANCIAL POLICIES AND EXCHANGE-RATE BEHAVIOUR

This chapter continues the assessment of monetary stabilization policy by looking at its effects on the exchange rate. The analysis is based on a review of the evolution of the exchange system to the present situation, where the rouble is convertible for current account transactions. In this light, it is possible to assess to what extent and in what way monetary factors affect the exchange rate; and, in turn, to assess how the exchange rate and the financial markets have by 1995 became fully operative in the management of monetary and fiscal policy.

5.1. Towards the unification of the exchange rate, 1989–July 1992

Liberalization of the exchange system began in the late 1980s when enterprises were first permitted to retain foreign exchange for imports, and to trade without the intermediation of the foreign trade organizations. In 1989, Vneshekonombank (VEB) monopoly in currency transactions was abolished, and in November 1989 currency auctions were introduced (Goldberg, 1992, p. 3); they were not, however, open to all agents. On 22 July 1990 internal trade in foreign currencies was legalized, and in November 1990 a commercial exchange rate replaced the official exchange rate for most transactions. This commercial rate was fixed in terms of a basket of currencies and set at a level three times as depreciated as the official exchange rate (Koen and Meyermans, 1994, p. 2). The system of auctions ended on 9 April 1991 with the creation of the Moscow Currency Exchange (MICEX), which operated through interbank transactions in foreign exchange. This simplified the previous system by which currency transactions took place according to a complex system of fixed exchange coefficients which varied across goods and regions (Goldberg, 1992, p. 6). On 2 January 1992 a dual exchange-rate system for current-account operators was officially introduced, comprising the market rate and a special commercial rate.

Until the unification of the exchange rate in July 1992 numerous different exchange rates remained in force (see Table 5.1).

- The special exchange rate (R55:US$1) applied to the 40% surrender requirement on raw materials. Regulations covering foreign currency export earnings were set out in a presidential decree of 30 December 1991. The decree provided for the mandatory sale to the hard-currency reserve of 40% of export earnings at a commercial rate in respect of exports of certain listed goods (mainly raw materials and their products) and services (transport, freight, financial and tourism). This revenue was to be used to service foreign debt, to stabilize the rouble market rate and to purchase necessary imports.
- The quasi-market rate applied to the 10% surrender imposed on all exports. The decree of 30 December 1991 also provided for the mandatory sale at the market rate of 10% of all export earnings into a hard-currency stabilization fund, to be used to maintain the rouble's market rate. This meant that certain exporters, notably of raw materials, had to sell 40% of their hard-currency earnings to the government at the special exchange rate of R55:US$1 and another 10% at the then market exchange rate. The government deposited this hard currency in a special account for servicing the foreign debt. The remaining foreign exchange was used by the exporter either to finance its own imports or to sell on the exchange market.
- The tourist rate was set in November 1989 at a level 10 times more depreciated than the official rate (McKinnon, 1991, p. 64). In December 1991, Gosbank abolished the fixed but adjustable tourist exchange rate of R47:US$1; until February 1992 it was basically a market rate.
- The exchange rate fixed at the Russian Exchange Bank reflected the exchange rate decided between firms for transactions taking place through the banks.
- The interbank rate, set weekly, was continued from January 1992 under the auspices of MICEX. MICEX was established in March 1991 as a joint stock company, founded by 25 banks with its membership rising to 32 Russian banks (including the CBR) plus the association of Russian banks and the Moscow government in January 1992. Auctions were held twice a week. Until January 1993 (when a

Table 5.1. Exchange-rate developments, December 1991–March 1992 (roubles per US dollar)

	Special commercial rate	Quasi-market rate	Market exchange rates[a]		
			Interbank market	Russian exchange bank[b]	Tourist exchange rate[c]
December 1991					
1–6	1.7		110	132	
7–14	1.7		170	172	101
15–21	1.7		170	144	115
22–31	1.7		169	144	108
January 1992					
2–6	55	110	150	144	109
7–14	55	110	180	178	114
15–21	55	110	230	120	116
22–31	55	110	230		120
February 1992					
1–6	55	110	225		126
7–14	55	110	210		117
15–21	55	100	170		99
22–29	55	90			
March 1992					
1–6	55	90	140		
7–14	55	90	140		
15–21	55	90	161		
22–31	55	100	160		

[a] The inter-enterprise exchange rates recorded by the banks are also market-determined rates but are difficult to interpret because of side payments which imply that the exchange rate does not reflect the price of the transaction.

[b] During an 'open auction' (i.e. an auction in which the Russian Exchange Bank was the only seller) held on 7 January the average exchange rate was R146 per US dollar. The exchange rates quoted in this table refer to the so-called 'closed auctions' where all legal persons (both residents and non-residents) could participate as buyers and sellers of foreign exchange. The auctions were discontinued from the fourth week of January 1992.

[c] Average mid-point of buying and selling rates in Moscow as published by *Commersant*.

Source: IMF (1992a), Table 26, p. 79.

weekly DM auction was introduced) it offered spot trading in dollars only.

- The exchange rate for centralized import operations was R5.4:US$1. Centralized imports were mainly of grains, medicines and some other basic consumer and producer goods.
- The exchange rate used for tax payments of Russian citizens with incomes in hard currency was R10:US$1.

The process of exchange-rate liberalization took the following form. On 1 July 1992 the CBR introduced a unified floating exchange rate at R125.26 to the dollar,[1] cancelling the special commercial rate (R55:US$1) and the quasi-market rate. The exchange rate was initially determined twice a week (Tuesday and Thursday) by trading on MICEX and was used as the official exchange rate by the Central Bank.[2] The new exchange rate applied to the state budget's revenue and expenditure accounts, to all kinds of state accounting with enterprises and households, and for book-keeping and taxation purposes. From June 1993 the exchange rate was quoted five times a week. Current-account convertibility for residents was formally introduced in November 1992 (IMF, 1993a, p. 35).

Apart from central import subsidies, there was therefore a single rouble exchange rate. The exchange rate was referred to by the CBR as applying to 'the rouble of the Russian Federation' rather than 'the rouble'. This denoted Russia's assertion of the right to control monetary policy in the rouble zone (Granville, 1992, 1994).

Another important reform initiated by the CBR that was linked to the unification of the exchange rate was to require exporters in the period 1 July–1 October 1992 to sell 30% of their hard-currency earnings to the CBR's currency reserve at a rate quoted by the CBR,[3] and to permit exporters to sell a further 20% freely on the interbank market. This greatly enhanced exports, since exporters were no longer subject to the surrender requirement at an appreciated exchange rate. However, they were still taxed in the sense that the CBR converted the dollars at the rate of exchange on the day of transaction, after which quite a long time could pass before the CBR paid over the roubles to the enterprise. In July 1993 the regulation was changed and firms were allowed to sell directly (through commercial banks) 50% of their export earnings (within 14 days of repatriation) on MICEX at the spot rate. The requirement to repatriate all export earnings immediately from receipts remains formally in effect.

Figure 5.1. Volume traded on MICEX, January 1992–December 1994 (monthly totals, US$m)

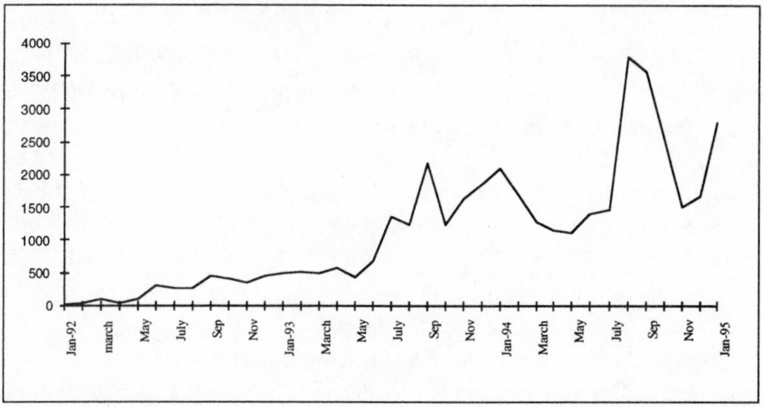

Source: Appendix 1, Table A.13.

Other reforms were implemented in 1993.[4] These included the authorization for banks to hold general licences freely to import and export foreign-currency banknotes, Treasury notes, coins and securities (April 1993); the introduction of a limit on open foreign-exchange positions of commercial banks (28 May 1993); authorization for non-residents to open rouble accounts in Russian banks and to sell hard currency on MICEX (15 July 1993); and authorization for non-residents to buy hard currency on MICEX (1 September 1993).

During the first months of 1992, the volume of transactions on the interbank market for foreign exchange was relatively small (see Figure 5.1). This was not because of the small number of trading participants but mainly because firms received huge centralized credits at negative real interest rates, so had no need to go to MICEX to convert the 50% of their foreign earnings that was not subject to obligatory conversion, especially given the low interest rate on rouble deposits. However, from this embryonic beginning transactions on the MICEX developed quite rapidly. By 1 July 1992 the number of trading participants reached 51 and by mid-1993 almost 70 banks were registered. At the end of 1994, transactions amounted to about 20% of all exchange transactions (about $500 million per day) (Johnson and White, 1995), the rest being directly traded between banks.[5]

5.2. The different exchange-rate regimes

Since 1992 the exchange rate has not been formally fixed. Instead, the policy has been to smooth the nominal exchange-rate depreciation. Interventions (in US dollars or roubles) from the CBR through MICEX have all been substantial over the whole period. According to Koen and Meyermans (1994, p. 7): 'Following exchange rate unification, the share of CBR intervention in total MICEX turnover remained large, averaging one third if measured by monthly net totals'. The Ministry of Finance also intervened, since it held some of the reserves in the form of gold and foreign exchange acquired through the centralized export scheme, an inheritance designed quite misguidedly to guarantee the authorities access to foreign exchange for debt service and 'essential' (centralized) imports.

During the first months of 1992, when expectations were high that an exchange stabilization fund of the Polish type would be available for Russia, a fixed exchange-rate regime was discussed and was expected to be adopted with the nominal exchange rate pegged to the dollar. Discussion at the time pointed to an exchange rate fixed at around R80 to the dollar. As a result, the nominal exchange rate appreciated substantially (Figures 5.2, 5.4), supported by an increase in the CBR refinance rate (Figure 5.3) as well as by CBR interventions (Koen and Meyermans, 1994, p. 8).

In the second half of 1992, when it became clear that a stabilization fund was not imminent and monetary policy was loosened, the nominal exchange rate started to depreciate substantially. Foreign advisers (for example, Sachs and Fisher) continued to advocate a fixed peg, but realistic prospects of this faded away. From about mid-1992 to mid-1993 the nominal exchange rate depreciated substantially (Figure 5.5) amid bleak expectations of future economic policy, with markets losing confidence in the government's ability to curb inflation.

High inflation combined with a relatively moderate depreciation of the nominal exchange rate meant a substantial appreciation of the real rate. During the first five months of 1993, the nominal average exchange rate of the rouble depreciated by 91% while prices rose by 164% during the period; as such the real exchange rate rose sharply (Figure 5.6). A turning-point came at the end of May 1993 when the IMF reached agreement with the government and CBR on a \$1.5 billion credit under the Fund's Systemic Transformation Facility (STF). With the ensuing increase in the CBR base rate (up to 210%, i.e. 17.5% per month), a major shift in market expectations occurred (Figure 5.7).

Figure 5.2. Nominal exchange rates, first half of 1992

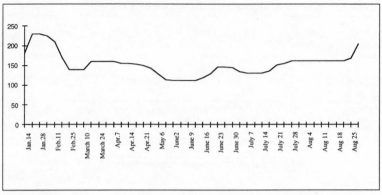

Source: MICEX.

Figure 5.3. Evolution of the inflation rate, the interbank interest rate and the refinance rate from February to July 1992

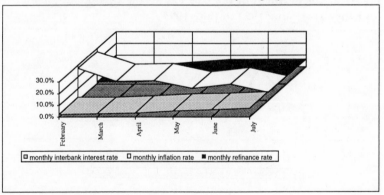

Source: Appendix 1, Tables A.9 and A.14.

By the end of 1993, the policy adopted by the government was to try to limit the fall in the rouble–dollar exchange rate to half the rate of inflation (Figure 5.8). Following the agreement with the IMF, the nominal exchange rate appreciated by 7% in July 1993 owing to the continuing increase in real interest rates. In July–August, the exchange rate remained around R1,000:US$1, the market pressure being for it to appreciate had the CBR not intervened to keep to this target.[6] With the Central Bank thus buying

Figure 5.4. Movement of the CPI and of the average nominal exchange rate in % during the first half of 1992

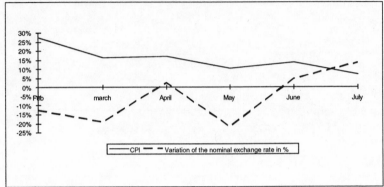

Source: Appendix 1, Table A.16.

Figure 5.5. Movement of the CPI and of the average nominal exchange rate, June 1992 to June 1993

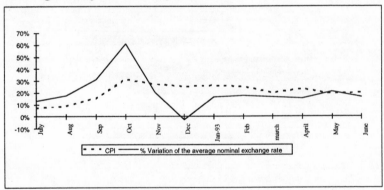

Source: Appendix 1, Table A.16.

considerable amounts of dollars on the exchange market, net international reserves increased substantially during the summer of 1993 (Figure 5.9). Also, as noted previously, the volume of trade was expanding rapidly during 1993, both in absolute terms and in the percentage of the total accounted for by exports (section 5.3). Political events in September–October 1993, however,

Figure 5.6. Exchange rates, mid-1992 to mid-1993, the average nominal exchange rate and the real exchange rate (July 1992 = 100)

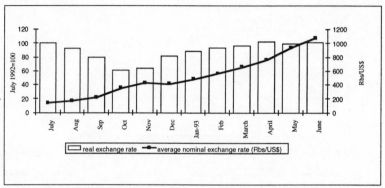

Source: MICEX, author's own calculations.

Figure 5.7. Real interest rates in % per month, 1992–4

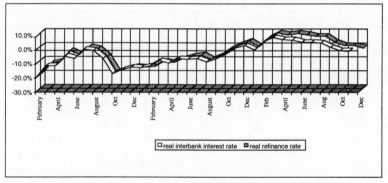

Note: The nominal interest rate is calculated in the Russian fashion, i.e. the annual percentage rate (APR) divided by 12 months ($n/12$) and the real interest rate is

$$R = \frac{1 + n/12}{1 + \pi} - 1$$

Source: calculated from Tables A.9 and A.14, Appendix 1.

brought a renewed sharp depreciation; subsequently, from October to December, the rate was relatively stable, falling by 10% a month while the inflation rate averaged 16% a month.

Figure 5.8. Movement of the CPI and of the nominal exchange rate, second half of 1993

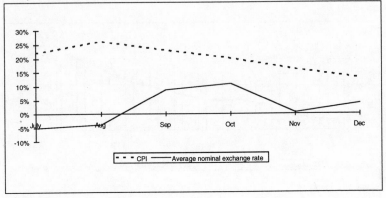

Source: Appendix 1, Table A.16.

Figure 5.9. Movement of net international reserves, May 1993 to January 1994 (Rbn)

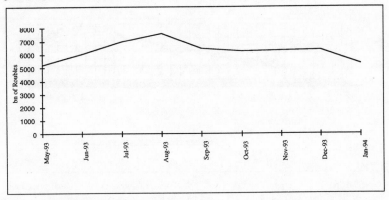

Source: Appendix 1, Table A.15.

From June 1993 to the autumn, the rouble remained stable while inflation continued at a rate of more than 20%. As a consequence the real exchange rate appreciated by nearly 100% – in other words, Russia's competitiveness fell by half.

Figure 5.10. The average wage in US dollars, 1992–4

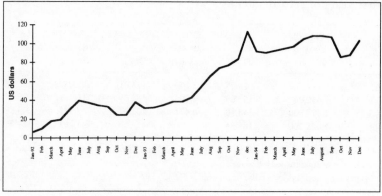

Source: Calculated from Tables A.8 and A.13, Appendix 1.

To show the appreciation of the exchange rate one can look at the evolution of Russian nominal wages, expressed in dollars (Figure 5.10), and compare the situation with that in Poland or the former CSFR at the equivalent stage of reform. Productivity may be assumed to be roughly identical, although Russian civilian industry was arguably less competitive internationally. From June 1992 until June 1993, the average monthly wage rate remained at about $40. By October 1993 it had doubled to $82, but was still considerably below the levels reached after 18 months of liberalization (the equivalent time) in Poland ($148) or Czechoslovakia ($161). In December 1993 the average wage was equivalent to $110; in December 1994 it was back to about $90. If we assume that average nominal wages can be used as an indicator (wages differ quite widely between sectors), a comparison of the dollar equivalent of Russian average nominal wages in 1992 and 1993 with those of Poland and the CSFR in their respective years of reform (Table 5.2) suggests that the rouble was undervalued.[7]

Following the setback to the reformers at the December 1993 elections, and the resignation from the government of Gaidar and Fedorov, the nominal exchange rate depreciated by 16% in January 1994, which was basically in line with the January 1994 inflation rate of 17.9% (Figure 5.11).

From Figure 5.11 the effect of inflation on the exchange rate is seen more clearly by calculating the real exchange rate. Taking July 1992 as base we see

Table 5.2. Cross-country comparison of average monthly wages in first years of reform, 1990–93

Months	Poland[a] nominal (zlotys)[d]	Dollar[e]	CSFR[b] nominal (koruny)[d]	Dollar	Russia[c] nominal (rouble)[f]	Dollar
6	912,500	96.05	3,600	116.01	5,067	35.18
12	1,460,000	153.68	4,566	164.0	16,071	38.77
18	1,697,900	148.18	4,491	161.02	47,371	44.68
24	2,045,000	186.64			141,283	114.0

[a] Wages for Poland: basically the same as the CSFR. From 1992, average earnings are net of income tax deductions for individuals.

[b] Wages for the CSFR: since the beginning of 1991, all economic units with more than 100 employees are covered. The data reflects monthly average earnings per worker. The series include wages, benefits and grants.

[c] Average monthly wages for Russia are net of benefits so another 20% should be added in order to be fully comparable with the figures for Poland and the CSFR. Even with this correction some room is left for the exchange rate to appreciate.

[d] Nominal wage from OECD (1992a).

[e] Wage in dollars using the official exchange rate. The exchange rates for Poland and the CSFR are from IMF, *International Statistics*. The exchange rates for Russia are calculated from MICEX.

[f] Goskomstat.

that the real exchange rate regained the July 1992 level in March 1993, and from July 1993 onwards started to appreciate sharply due to the high inflation rate and the relatively small depreciation of the nominal exchange rate. The latter more or less stabilized in the range of R1,000 to the dollar from May 1993 to September 1993, while inflation rates peaked at 26% a month in August 1993. During the second half of 1993, the nominal exchange rate depreciated by less than 20% while monthly domestic consumer price inflation averaged 20%. At the same time, real rouble money contracted sharply, while gross CBR foreign-exchange reserves surged in the third quarter and declined somewhat in the fourth. With increasingly positive interest rates and the expectation of a lower inflation rate, the real exchange rate appreciated sharply.

In the first half of 1994, the rouble fell against the US dollar at a slower rate than domestic inflation, except in March. By the end of June 1994 the rouble had lost almost 60% of its nominal value (taking the average monthly exchange rate) compared with an inflation rate of 72% for the period. So again the exchange rate appreciated in real terms.

Figure 5.11. Average nominal and real exchange rate *vis-à-vis* the US dollar, 1992–4 (index July 1992 = 100)

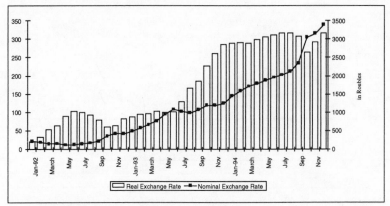

Source: Appendix1, Table A.13, author's own calculations.

Figure 5.12. CBR intervention in million of US dollars

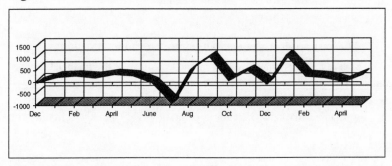

Source: Appendix 1, Table A.13.

Throughout the whole period (1992–4) the rouble was supported by intervention of the CBR (totalling about US$1.4 billion for Q1 1994) (Figure 5.12). The system in place was designed to smooth the nominal exchange-rate depreciation with regard to the inflation rate (Figure 5.13). However, after the 'Black Tuesday' rouble crash (11 October 1994), the CBR intervened heavily in order to bring the real exchange rate in December 1994 back roughly to its September level. This collapse was called 'Black Tuesday' because of the rouble's plunge to R3,926 per US dollar from R3,081 – a 27%

Figure 5.13. Monthly movements of the CPI and the nominal exchange rate, December 1993 to December 1994 (%)

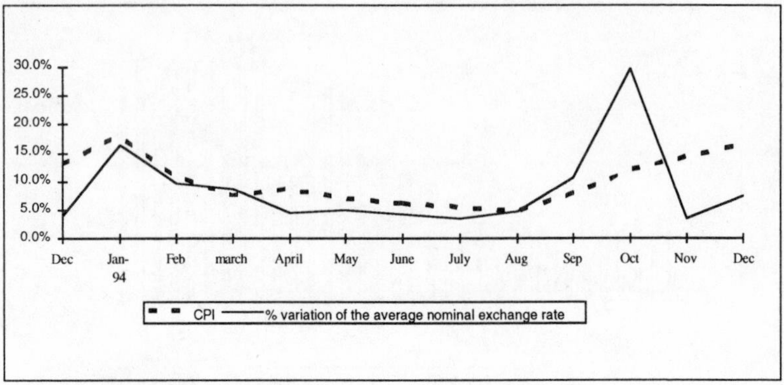

Source: Appendix 1, Table A.16.

decline in one day. The event seriously disrupted Russia's financial markets and threatened the path of economic stability.

5.3. The response of the exchange rate to monetary policy

The path of the exchange rate reflects the evolution of the financial strategy pursued by the authorities. Black Tuesday was not an accident. It reflected a combination of weak fiscal policy and loose monetary policy in the context of new financial markets where money can move very quickly from one asset to another.

Monetary expansion and the exchange rate

We saw earlier that a government can finance its budget deficit domestically in two ways: by selling bonds or by printing money. By printing money, the Central Bank increases the stock of base money. In Russia, this was mostly done by directly allocating credits from the Central Bank. Credit auctions represented a small though growing share. (However, in February 1995 credits from the CBR for the purpose of budget financing were banned.) The exchange rate is determined by monetary equilibrium. The exchange rate and prices do not move at the same rate. When monetary expansion pushes down interest rates, the exchange rate adjusts immediately. An excess supply of

Figure 5.14. Effect of the expansion of rouble M2 on the exchange rate (appreciation: down), January 1992 to November 1994

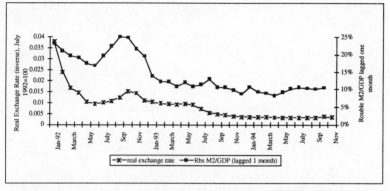

Source: This figure (although with April 1991 as base) was produced by Easterly and Vieira da Cunha (1993). They explained (pp. 18-9) that 'Since the domestic price index appears in the denominator of both M2/GDP and the real exchange rate, what figure 3 is really showing is the correlation between nominal rouble M2 and the nominal exchange rate.' CBR data and MICEX.

money implies a corresponding excess demand for foreign exchange. The rouble exchange rate responded to the variations of the money supply: that is, an increase/decrease in the rouble money supply led to a depreciation/ appreciation of the rouble (Figure 5.14). Failing CBR intervention, the exchange rate depreciates/appreciates until equilibrium is restored.

Figure 5.14 shows the correlation between M2 and the nominal exchange rate. It is suggested that the exchange rate responds to the movement of rouble M2 with no more than a one-month lag (the lag of one month reflects the period of at least two weeks needed for government credits to reach MICEX). That is, any additional increment or shortfall in monetary balances is used almost immediately to buy or sell foreign exchange, leading to either a depreciation or an appreciation of the nominal exchange rate.

We can see from Figure 5.14 that the relation held quite steady, albeit with some exceptions – as for instance during the summer of 1993 when, as the result of the relative credit tightening and the adjusted interest differential described below, it became profitable to convert foreign-exchange deposits into rouble deposits, generating upward pressure on the exchange rate. The CBR responded by intervening extensively to keep the nominal exchange rate relatively stable; but in doing so it bought a large quantity of foreign exchange, which meant injecting roubles into the economy, thus contributing to a persistently very high inflation rate of 20% per month on average.

Does the exchange rate really matter?
The exchange-rate level can be inflationary or deflationary in two ways: through its effect on the internal price of tradeable goods, including foodstuffs, energy, and other raw materials; and through the budget: if the exchange rate is undervalued, this will raise the domestic cost of servicing foreign debt – but it will also raise the value of tariff revenue; if the exchange rate is overvalued, this will reduce revenues from tariffs since the domestic price of imports will be lower (Hansson, 1991a), but it will also lower the domestic cost of foreign debt service.

However, if we estimate the relation between the exchange rate lagged by one month and the rate of inflation for the whole period 1992–4, no correlation is to be found. An explanation for the lack of correlation was suggested by Easterly and Vieira da Cunha (1993, pp. 19–20): 'The lack of direct effect between changes in the exchange rate and price formation can be traced to remaining institutional rigidities, notably the still highly distorted foreign trading system and the thinness of the foreign currency markets outside the main metropolitan areas. Especially in 1992 the huge volume of import subsidies effectively insulated vast segments of the economy from changes in the exchange rate.'

The exchange rate had a very limited effect on the balance of trade until the end of 1994.

Imports
In the early stages of reform, the large fraction of imports still centrally purchased did not respond to the exchange rate. In 1992, 60% of imports were subsidized (medicine, meat, cereals). Consequently imports, despite the appreciation of the exchange rate in real terms, decreased substantially over the three years, reflecting the sharp cut in 1993 of centralized imports and their final abolition in 1994 (Table 5.6). Centralized imports decreased from US$10.5 bn in 1992 to US$5.3 bn in 1993; import subsidies declined from 11.9% of GDP in 1992 to 2.3% of GDP in 1993 (see Table 4.8); the

Table 5.6. Imports with non-FSR (US$ bn)

	1992	1993[a]	1994[b]
Imports	−37.2	−34.3	−35.7
Unadjusted[c]	−37.2	−24.8	
Food and light industry	−8.3	−8.1	
Machinery and equipment	−16.2	−9.8	
Humanitarian imports	−1.9	−0.3	
Other[d]	−10.8	−5.9	
Adjustment		−9.6	

[a] Revised estimates.

[b] Preliminary estimates from Goskomstat.

[c] Excludes trade with Baltic states and includes a cost, insurance, freight/free on board adjustment factor.

[d] Excludes trade with Baltic states.

Sources: IMF (1995), Table 41, p. 102 for 1992 and 1993; Goskomstat RF, *Russian Statistical Yearbook* for 1994, p. 72.

disbursement of bilateral credit shrank by 56% in 1993 and humanitarian imports declined from US$1.9 bn to US$0.3 bn (IMF, 1995, p. 40).

As stressed by Sarafanov (1995, p. 241), 'the main cause of the decline in imports was the reduction of so-called centralised critical imports due to the immense federal budget deficit and the insufficient means to continue subsidising the import of food, medicines, and raw materials at the 1992 level'. Imports are freed from quotas and licences (except for security and health reasons). Moreover, for the first half of 1992 no customs tariffs were in effect. Import tariffs were introduced in the second half of 1992 for fiscal reasons and yielded about R0.1 trillion in 1992, or 0.3% of GDP and R0.9 trillion in 1993, that is, 0.6% of GDP (IMF, 1995, Table 25, p. 86) instead of the respective forecasts of R2.5 trillion and R4.5 trillion (Sarafanov, 1995, p. 243). These somewhat lower yields were due to 'tariff exemptions for many enterprises and regions' (Sarafanov, 1995, p. 243).

As shown by Drebentsov (1995, pp. 175–91), import tariffs were increased several times (Table 5.7) but were not really conceived and did not act as a barrier to trade. Only in March 1994 and subsequently in July 1995 when import duties of 10% and 30% were introduced on imported food – on top of a 10% and 20% VAT, introduced in April 1995 – can one say that duties

Table 5.7. Import tariffs between 1992 and 1995 (%)

	Average unweighted	Rate weighted by 1992 imports	Rate weighted by 1993 imports[a]
January–June 1992	0	0	
July–August 1992	3.95	3.81	
September 1992–March 1993	11.46	10.71	11.05
April 1993–1 July 1994	9.51	8.67	9.23
July 1994–July 1995	15.52	12.82	14.13

[a] First three quarters of 1993.
Source: Drebentsov (1995), p. 181.

were imposed as a protectionist answer to the appreciated rouble rate. The prospect of joining the World Trade Organization (WTO) should prevent further protective measures, especially since, in the case of food, tariffs failed to protect farmers and managed only to reinforce profits of domestic food processing and retailing monopolies.

VAT on imports was introduced in February 1993, but here too this did not represent a barrier to trade since many exemptions were granted. According to the IMF (1995, p. 15), 'the VAT on imports yielded only about 5% of total revenues, whereas a level of around 30% is not uncommon in other countries'.

This means that given the fraction of non-centralized imports and the abolition of centralized credits, imports were responding to the exchange rate. Increases in imports were especially substantial in light industrial products. In the second half of 1993, imports increased from US$16 bn to US$18.4 bn (Table 5.8) – that is, a 15% increase – while exports increased by 11.4%. This reflected the 150% real appreciation of the rouble.

Exports

The system of export licences and quotas (the latter determining the proportion of domestic production that can be exported), especially on oil, explained why, during 1992, despite the highly depreciated exchange rate, no export surge was observed. 'In June and December 1993, and in the face of declining export competitiveness, the Government removed the export quota requirement on a range of products, including timber, fertilisers, coal and meat products.' (IMF,

Table 5.8. Total exports and imports growth with non–FSR, 1993[a], in US$bn and % change

	HI	H2	% change
Exports	21.9	24.4	11.42%
Unadjusted[b]	18.7	24.2	29.41%
Oil	6	5.9	−1.67%
Natural gas[c]	3.5	3.5	0.00%
Gold	0.3	0.8	166.67%
Other	8.9	14.2	59.55%
Adjustments	3.2	0.2	−93.75%
Imports	−16	−18.4	15.00%
Unadjusted	−11.8	−13	10.17%
Food and light industry	−3.9	−4.2	7.69%
Machinery and equipment	−4.5	−5.4	20.00%
Humanitarian imports	−0.7	−1.2	71.43%
Other[b]	−2.9	−3	3.45%
Adjustment	−4.2	−5.4	28.57%

[a] Revised estimates.
[b] Excludes trade with Baltic states.
[c] Includes valuation adjustment associated with Yamburg agreement.
Source: IMF (1995), Table 41, p. 102.

1995, p. 51) But while oil and natural gas constitute 50% of Russian exports, oil export quotas were officially abolished only on 1 January 1995.[8]

Moreover various restrictions are imposed by other countries on Russian exports (e.g. uranium, steel, textiles, aluminium and high-tech goods). As pointed out by the IMF (1993b, p. 41), 'in 1992, for instance there were about 20 anti-dumping procedures (Uranium from the USA, carbamide, copper sulphate, potassium chloride, etc. from the EC) in progress against Russian goods and the loss of Russian exports due to existing Western barriers was comparable in monetary terms with the amount of bilateral credits provided by the West in 1992 i.e. more than $1bn'. However if, as planned, Russia becomes a full member of the WTO, restrictions of this kind on Russian exports will have to be more controlled.

New rates of export duties on a number of goods and services came into force on 1 July 1992. The duties are assessed in ECU per unit of weight of the goods or as a percentage of the dutiable value of the goods and services.

Table 5.9. Exports with non–FSR (US$ bn)

	1992	1993[a]	1994[b]
Exports	41.6	46.3	48
Unadjusted[c]	41.6	42.9	
Oil	12.7	11.8	
Natural gas[d]	7.5	6.9	
Gold	1.1	1	
Other	20.3	23.1	
Adjustments		3.4	

[a] Revised estimates.

[b] Preliminary estimates from Goskomstat.

[c] Excludes trade with Baltic states.

[d] Includes valuation adjustment associated with Yamburg agreement.

Sources: IMF (1995), Table 41, p. 102 for 1992 and 1993; Goskomstat, *Russian Statistical Yearbook* for 1994, p. 72.

As part of the trend towards liberalization of exports, export duties were revised several times (January 1993, November 1993 and January 1995). For instance, tariffs on oil exports were cut from 30 ECUs per tonne ($37) to 23 ECUs ($28) per tonne in January 1995. But as emphasized by Drebentsov (1995, p. 193) this process of export liberalization has been erratic; for instance, 'the number of commodity groups subject to export taxation rose from 30 in January to 70 in July 1992 and then decreased to 53 in January 1993 and to 29 in November 1993'. Export duties yielded R0.3 trn in 1992 (1.7% of GDP) and R4.3 trn in 1993 (2.7% of GDP)' (IMF, 1995, Table 25, p. 86).

Because of the export quotas, exports fell in 1992 from US$51 bn in 1991 (IMF, 1993a, Table 26, p. 107) to US$41.6 bn (Table 5.9, above) despite the sharp depreciation of the exchange rate. However, statistics on foreign trade need to be treated with caution; they are even less statistically sound than other statistics. Whenever possible, IMF figures have been used. The Ministry of Economic Relations (MFER) and Goskomstat figures produce conflicting foreign trade statistics.[9] Underreporting (Sutela, 1995, p. 92) and smuggling following the dissolution of the Soviet Union were substantial in 1992. Also exports of many goods decreased at current prices but, measured at constant prices, actually increased.[10]

In 1993, the current account with countries outside the former Soviet Union was brought into surplus of US$2.3 bn in 1993, compared with a

Table 5.10. Current account with non–FSR (US$ bn)

	1992	1993[a]	QI 1994	1994[b]
Current account	−5.7	2.3	−0.9	
Trade balance	4.4	12	1.7	12.3
Exports	41.6	46.3	9.1	48
Imports	−37.2	−34.3	−7.4	−35.7
Services, net	−10.1	−9.7	−2.6	
Non-factor sevices, net	−5.5	−5.3	−1.4	
Travel and tourism	−0.4	−1.4	−0.4	
Interest, net	−4.6	−4.3	−1.2	
Receipts	0.9	0.7	0.2	
Payments	−5.5	−5.1	−1.4	

[a] Revised estimates.
[b] Preliminary estimates from Goskomstat.
Sources: IMF (1995), Table 41, p. 102 for 1992, 1993 and Q1 1994; Goskomstat, *Russian Statistical Yearbook* for 1994, p. 72.

deficit of US$5.7 bn in 1992 (Table 5.10). As already mentioned, the reason is to be found not in an increase of exports but in the substantial reduction in centralized imports. With regard to the deficit on net services, there was a slight improvement in 1993, although 'the availability of detailed data on non-factor services improved somewhat in 1993, therefore previous years' data may not be strictly comparable' (IMF, 1995, p. 41). The IMF also emphasizes that no information is available on profits and labour remittances but they are believed to be small.

As was stressed in Chapter 4, in 1992 a large proportion of imports was financed by tied credits. Thus the decline in imports is closely connected with the reduction of tied credits, and the trade surplus in 1993 did not substantially improve the service of external debt but served mainly to lower the future debt service (IMF, 1995, p. 41).

In 1992, with an overall need for balance–of–payments financing totalling US$13.3 bn, and almost no international reserves, payment on the foreign debt was stopped altogether. In 1993 the financing need was still over US$14 bn but this time, as seen previously, the monetary authorities were able to accumulate US$3.4 bn by buying dollars on the MICEX during the second and third

Table 5.11. Balance-of-payments financing (US$ bn)

	1992	1993[a]	Q1 1994[b]
Current account	−5.7	2.3	−0.9
Capital account	−1.2	−10.1	−3.5
Errors and omissions[c]	−6.4	−6.5	−1.1
Overall balance	−13.3	−14.3	−5.4
Financing	−13.3	−14.3	−5.4
Net official international reserves	−0.8	−3.4	1.3
Convertible currency payments			
of countries of FSR[d]		0.4	0.2
Arrears	6.9	−2.7	
Official	3.8	−2.7	
Non-official	3.1		
Deferral of pre-cutoff principal	7.2	5.6	0.9
Official	1.6		
Non-official	5.6	5.6	0.9
Official rescheduling		11.2	1.9
Amount unpaid pending rescheduling		3.2	1.1

[a] Revised estimates.
[b] Preliminary estimates.
[c] Errors and omissions are thought to include both unrecorded current and capital operations.
[d] Use of convertible currency proceeds arising from payments between Russia and other countries of former Soviet Union.
Source: IMF (1995), Table 41, p.103 for 1992, 1993 and Q1 1994.

quarter of 1993 (Table 5.11). Nevertheless there was very little debt servicing in 1993. Russia's convertible debt stock stood at US$83.7 bn in 1993 compared with US$ 78.7 bn a year earlier: that is, about 26% of GDP (using the constant real exchange rate of the first half of 1994) as estimated by the IMF (1995, p. 47), or 122% of export of goods and non-factor services. But the short maturity structure of recent borrowing (about four years on average, with a one-year grace period) and the quantity of payments already overdue have resulted in significant cashflow difficulties. The debt service burden (i.e. current maturities on a commitment basis relative to total, worldwide exports of goods and services) was 29% in 1993 compared with 25% in 1992. Cash payments amounted to an estimated $2.5 bn mostly to a group of official creditors in the context of the agreement signed on April 2 1993 in Paris. The remaining debt-service obligations either were rescheduled or were in arrears pending discussions on debt rescheduling.' (IMF, 1995, p. 47) For 1994, only preliminary estimates for the first quarter are available; they show an overall financing need of US$5.4 bn. According to Goskomstat, quoted in *Russian Economic Trends* (1994, vol. 3, no. 4, pp. 79–80), foreign debt was estimated at the end of 1994 at US$91 bn and total debt service at US$32.5 bn of which only US$3.7 bn was paid during the first three quarters of 1994. During the first quarter, the level of international reserves fell by US$1.3 bn and at the end of November 1994, international reserves stand at US$4.1 bn.

Black Tuesday: a proof that markets are working

Residents hold interest-bearing assets denominated in roubles and in US dollars. Relative yields determine the portfolio shares of rouble assets and of US dollar assets converted into roubles at the spot exchange rate. Residents will seek an additional amount of financial assets denominated in roubles when they expect the currency to appreciate or when the domestic interest rate increases relative to the foreign interest rate (this variation, in its pure form, would depend on there being no risk differential).

The exchange rate clears the foreign-exchange market through its impact on the expected return and the stock of assets denominated in foreign currency. Exchange-rate expectations are driven by the perceived divergence between the spot and the long-run equilibrium rate (Koen and Meyermans, 1994).[11] Agents base their expectations of the long-run price level on recently observed price movements.

Movements in and out of the domestic currency are described by equation (5.1):

(5.1)   adjusted interest differential $= i - i_f - de/e$

where i is the monthly interest rate on the rouble interbank market or bonds, i_f the monthly interest rate on foreign exchange deposits and de/e the monthly rate of depreciation of the nominal rate of exchange (negative in case of an appreciation).

This relationship, as shown in Table A.14, Appendix 1, takes into consideration the interest differentials on foreign and interest-bearing rouble assets, assuming a 0.5% monthly interest rate on foreign exchange (here dollar) deposits,[12] and the rate of depreciation/appreciation of the rouble to the dollar. According to this relation, the movements in and out of rouble deposits can be predicted. It is assumed that the difference in interest rates between rouble and dollar interest-bearing assets reflects the difference in inflation rates and that this is also reflected in the movement of the exchange rate. The basic assumption is that the inflation differential between, say, Russia and the United States is matched by the depreciation or the appreciation of the Russian rouble.

When, as a result of positive real interest rates on rouble assets, it was more profitable to invest in roubles than in dollars, this contributed to the appreciation in real terms of the exchange rate. For instance, in August 1994 the APR interbank lending rate on one to three months (Appendix 1, Table A.14) was 124% yearly, which means a rate of about 10% per month, while the inflation rate was 4.6%; the exchange rate was depreciating at around 7% per month and the interest rate on dollar deposits stood at about 0.5% per month. Consequently (according to equation 5.1) it was more profitable to invest in roubles than in dollars. But in September 1994, as Table A.14 shows, it became more profitable to invest in dollars: the monthly interbank lending rate was about 10%, while the rate of depreciation was 19%. The decision to lower the refinance rate at the end of August 1994 (see Appendix 1, Table A.3) was a mistake.

With regard to bonds,[13] the annual yield on three-month Treasury bills is shown in Figure 5.15.[14] The public invested increasingly in bonds (Treasury bills) from May 1993 until August 1994. In this period, the rouble fell by about 100% and the government was able to outbid the dollar by offering 150% interest on its paper. The market grew so quickly that the debt could be serviced with the proceeds of new issues without the need to raise interest rates. After debt repayment, these bond issues generated net funds which could be used to cover part of the budget deficit.

Since autumn 1994, however, investment in dollars has offered a higher return than bonds (Figure 5.16). To attract investors, the government has been forced to offer yields of up to 500% per annum in real terms (Figure 5.15) in competition with the dollar, which has doubled its value against the rouble every six months. The market therefore stopped growing. New issues were barely sufficient to cover repayments of previous issues reaching maturity; only about 10% of new issues remained for the government to use. The interest cost of these bonds has become too high for this to be an effective means for financing the budget deficit.

Despite a declining inflation trend from January 1994 to August 1994 (the monthly inflation rate was at its lowest in August 1994 at 4.6%) and the high

Figure 5.15. Annual yield on three-month T-bills, 1993–4

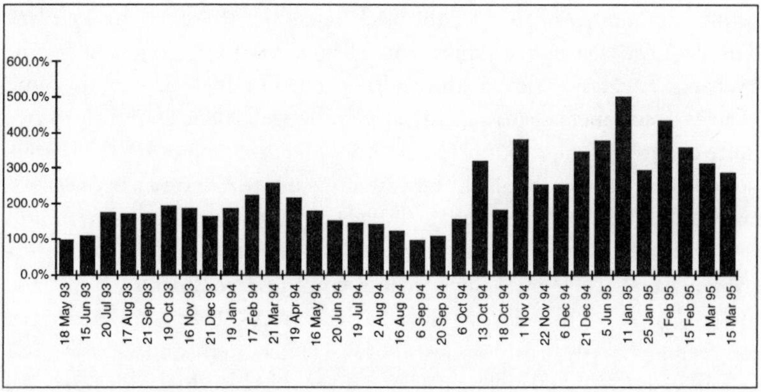

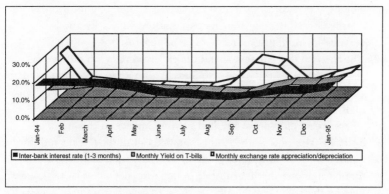

Source: MICEX (author's own calculations)

Figure 5.16. Monthly interbank interest rate, monthly yield on T-bills and monthly exchange-rate appreciation/depreciation in 1994 (%)

Sources: MICEX and CBR, author's own calculations.

Central Bank refinance rate, inflationary expectations remained very high. This was due to a large-scale slippage in the fiscal position accompanied by an expansion of credits from the Central Bank. The way the government dealt with the question (by developing arrears on public-sector payments) did not convince the market.

The mixture of this bad budget policy with a relaxation in credits in the spring and summer of 1994 led to 'Black Tuesday'.[15] In other words, 'Black Tuesday' was the perfect illustration of how monetary factors affect the exchange rate: the 27% fall in the exchange rate in a single day was the result of an excessive increase in M2 to finance the budget deficit, essentially to give more credits to the agriculture sector. From March to August 1994, M2 grew between 7% and 18% while the rate of the exchange rate varied between 4% and 6% per month (Appendix 1, Table A.16). Also the CBR lowered its refinance rate from 155% per year to 130% per year on 23 August 1994 (Appendix 1, Table A.3). The savings bank and commercial banks also lowered most of their deposit rates. In September 1994 the CBR stopped intervening heavily, partly because the level of net international reserves was at its lowest (US$2,669 million in September 1994 compared with US$6,392 million in June 1994; see Figure 5.17) and partly because some industrial lobbies were complaining about the 'overvaluation' of the exchange rate.

In sum, 'Black Tuesday' was the market response to serious failings in governmental policy:

(1) The fiscal position contributed extensively to building inflationary expectations. These inflationary expectations were taken up by a versatile financial market ready to take high-risk positions.
(2) The interest-rate differential and the expected inflation differential clearly influenced the rouble/$US exchange rate in the short run. Also evident was market participants' awareness of the risks associated with high inflation.
(3) The increase of nominal M2 had a strong impact on the nominal exchange rate: that is, the credits pumped out in the second and third quarters of 1994, instead of going to their intended destination immediately (northern territories, agriculture, defence factories), were held by the commercial banks for them to switch from rouble assets to dollar assets following the respective interest rates.

In order to limit the risk of currency speculation, a certain number of measures were introduced at the beginning of 1995. These included a 10% limit on exchange-rate movements during the daily MICEX auction; a limit of 30% on the open position of banks; and the introduction of a 2% minimum reserve requirement on foreign-currency deposits (*Russian Economic Trends*, 1994, vol. 3, no. 4, p. 29).

Figure 5.17. Net international reserves, 1994 (US$m)

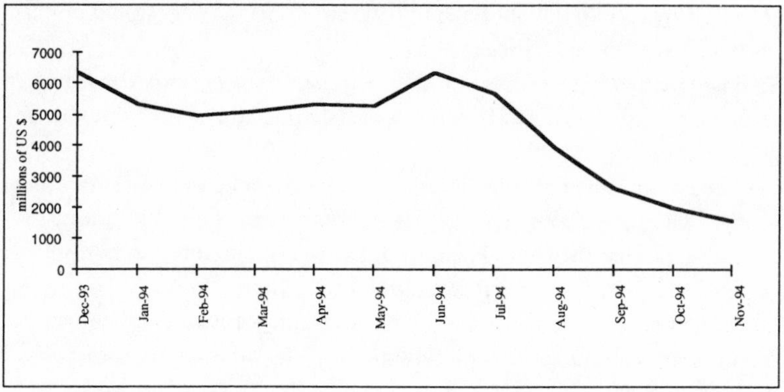

Source: Appendix 1, Table A.15.

The assessment of 'Black Tuesday' leads unavoidably back to the question set aside, as we have seen, after the initial phase of reform in 1992: to what extent would Russia benefit in present circumstances from the introduction of a fixed exchange-rate peg?

Advocates of a fixed peg argue that the adoption of an official parity prevents the monetary authorities from allowing excessive growth of the money supply, thereby imposing a degree of financial discipline. This discipline is absent if a country's currency floats freely and the domestic inflation rate is free to deviate permanently from that of its trading partners. Under a fixed exchange-rate regime, the monetary authorities are committed to a certain parity, while credit expansion is restricted by the availability of international reserves and the capacity to borrow internationally. If the authorities do not control the expansion of credit and therefore the way in which the budget deficit is financed, they will have to devalue and so lose credibility,[16] thus compromising the whole stabilization attempt. In the context of loose credit policies, an exchange-rate target would inevitably end in a succession of financial crises followed by devaluations. This would introduce a high degree of instability into the behaviour of the real exchange rate. This instability would in turn generate macroeconomic uncertainty and disrupt trade and investment flows.

If we look at the conditions for a fixed exchange rate, for instance as suggested by Williamson (1991), very few, if any, of them seem to correspond with the Russian situation. Williamson's conditions were:

(1) The country should be small relative to the rest of the world.
(2) The currency to which the country plans to peg its rate should be that of its main trading partner.
(3) The targeted inflation rate must match that of the country to which the currency is pegged. In other words, strong convergence should be the aim.
(4) The commitment to a fixed rate has to be credible, therefore the necessary institutional arrangements should be in place. This means, above all, that the central bank should be committed to the task and have the means to carry it through.
(5) In the presence of high elasticity of substitution between foreign and domestic currency, the economy may be left without a nominal anchor in a flexible exchange-rate regime. In this situation, and assuming that the necessary reserves or credibility are there to back the scheme, to choose the nominal exchange rate as an anchor is the right solution. The point is made still more strongly by Vegh (1992). He reviews various cases of hyperinflation from Europe after the First World War to the Bolivian episode of April 1984–September 1985, and claims that with exchange-rate stabilization, inflation is stopped almost immediately.

To defend the parity of the currency, a minimum share of the domestic money supply should be backed by foreign-exchange reserves. Lacking international reserves and access to international financing, Russia has so far been forced to adopt the only realistic option of a smooth exchange-rate float (depreciation). In the absence of an international exchange stabilization fund (similar to the Polish one), a flexible exchange rate is easiest to manage since the need for central bank interventions on the foreign-exchange market is reduced. However, there have been different exchange-rate episodes in the period since 1992. In 1994 (section 5.2), when the nominal exchange rate was adjusted in line with inflation, 'Black Tuesday' demonstrated to the authorities that a nominal depreciation is no substitute for bringing domestic monetary and fiscal policies under control. This event underlies the fact that from now on the Russian government has to take account of rapidly developing financial markets. Russia's market economy has reached a stage in its development where inflationary expectations from the private sector count, and these expectations depend on the fiscal and monetary policy followed by the Russian authorities – especially since the rouble is highly substitutable for the dollar, although the rouble was enforced officially as the sole tender on 1 January 1994.

If Russia had been in a position to finance exchange-rate intervention through foreign borrowing, as in Poland, it would have been able to peg the exchange rate at the beginning of the reform process. In a world of capital mobility, a fixed exchange rate requires Russia to be able to maintain fiscal discipline. Such a regime would countenance devaluation only in the face of external shocks beyond the authorities' control, not as an expedient to help the authorities overcome their own failures in the conduct of fiscal policy. The only response to such failures in the disciplined conditions of a pegged exchange rate would be a tough fiscal retrenchment unalleviated by any devaluation.

In Russia, three years into the reform programme, the use of the nominal exchange rate as an anchor is still under sporadic discussion and will probably remain so for quite some time.[17] Whether a fixed exchange rate would help to build credibility or whether, on the contrary, credibility is required in the Russian programme before the exchange rate can be fixed is far from clear. The uncertainty on this point means that the benefits for Russia of a fixed exchange rate remain an open question. Given the severe problems associated with overvaluation of the currency, it is difficult to take a strong position in support of greater rigidity of nominal exchange rates. Nevertheless, the arguments for some sort of peg retain their force: the load of external adjustment must be shared by both the exchange rate and financial policies. Although exchange-rate flexibility eases the process of adjustment to external shocks, the Russian government may find it desirable to build up a reputation for financial responsibility.

6 CONCLUSION

Judgments of success or failure depend on the basis of comparison. Comparing Russia today with an advanced industrial economy like Japan would clearly be absurd: but it would be misleading to pass a verdict on Russian economic reform even on the basis of comparison with the more advanced central European transition economies. Only in relation to the economic situation inherited by the Russian reformers at the moment the Soviet Union collapsed in December 1991 does the full extent of what has been achieved become clear.

A proper understanding of that inheritance must distinguish between the systemic failings of central planning and the breakdown of the period 1989–91 largely caused by pseudo-reformist measures of the Gorbachev administration. In the latter phase government actions largely left the old system in place while crippling its ability to deliver even the fragile equilibrium and minimal material benefits characteristic of the high Soviet period.

On the systemic side, Soviet-style central planning was incapable of delivering not only innovation and growth, but even price stability. Under the Soviet regime 'inflation' was characterized by increasing shortages and black markets. Enterprises hid price increases behind 'quality improvements' and government statistics showed only official prices (Nuti, 1986), disregarding the fact that many goods were not available at the official price, but only at a higher price in certain shops or on the black market.

However, the events of 1991 made the Russian reformers' predicament even worse. By the end of that year, the Gosbank's reserves had been exhausted; gold reserves had been dissipated; grain reserves were practically non-existent. The situation was encapsulated in the bankruptcy that December of the Vneshekonombank of the USSR – one of the biggest international financial scandals of the century, involving total default on liabilities including even short-term trade credit.

Seen in this perspective, the success of Russian economic reform consists above all in its very first step – price liberalization: a step which, for all its apparent radicalism, was in reality little more than a forced response to the monetary overhang and repressed inflation which underlay the disastrous late Soviet economic legacy. The political argument used by the Soviet authorities for not raising prices to their market-clearing level or freeing them altogether was that the distribution of wealth and income had to be egalitarian. However, this was a questionable argument even for basic goods like food:

> Slogans of social justice are often invoked against price increases, but the real benefits of price controls to the poor are often meagre. For example, in the Soviet Union the state allocations of meat were channelled almost exclusively to the cities, especially the main cities and elite groups within them. In 1987, Soviet families with per capita monthly incomes exceeding 150 roubles were reported to pay, on average, 31 percent less per kilogram of meat purchased than families with per capita monthly incomes of less than 50 roubles. When differences in the amounts of meat purchased are taken into account, higher-income families received three times the meat subsidies of lower-income families (*Izvestia*, 19 November 1987; Osband, 1992a, p. 686)

The benefits of price liberalization are obvious to anyone living in almost any large Russian city. Not only are the shops full and queues a thing of the past, but a whole trading and service sector has materialized with the removal of the state's monopoly on foreign trade. Free prices quickly ended shortages, releasing time spent queuing for labour efforts (see Lipton and Sachs, 1990; Boycko, 1991; Bennett, 1990).[1] One of the many indicators of the new world of consumer choice has been the gradual fading away of the foul odour characteristic of Soviet food shops.

On the producer level, the standard objection to the price liberalization policy is the existence of monopoly. But there is no direct connection between the relation which links monetary growth and inflation on the one hand and the degree of monopolization on the other (Blanchard and Layard, 1991). A monopoly can set its prices higher (a once-and-for-all jump) than they would have been in a competitive surrounding, but it cannot increase its prices continually every month. Once prices are freed and if the economy is opened (i.e. with current-account convertibility and low import tariffs) competition takes root, monopolies gradually lose power and prices will find their equilibrium level; and from the inflation point of view, the resulting cuts in subsidies have a positive effect on the size of the budget deficit.

In 1992, the only choice for Russia was to have either hidden and repressed inflation or open inflation; to have no inflation was not an option. In these circumstances, open inflation is a better alternative than persistent excess demand:

> If socialism, through a combination of bad luck and ill judgement, has failed to deliver price stability it is better to recognise it than to ignore this failure or treat it as a passing phenomenon. The persistence of excess demand, indeed the elevation of shortage to a systemic failure, leads to a prima facie case for suspecting that it is maintained primarily because it conceals the privileges of the elite through exclusive access to luxuries and necessities at abnormally low prices, while market-clearing prices would reveal and quantify privileges, as its maintenance would require drastically more unequal incomes and wealth. (Nuti, 1986, p. 76)

Enterprise management was decentralized without allowing unrestricted private ownership of capital goods.[2] This resulted in the relaxation of control over wages by firms which, as state-owned entities, still expected to receive the necessary financial support from the government to cover their wage-bills and other costs. Inflationary pressures followed from the demand side of the economy. In the absence of capital markets, households were not able to use their excess purchasing power for investment in innovative enterprises. Savings represented a forcibly delayed demand for consumer goods.

The debate on 'big bang' versus gradualism is not addressed here because it exaggerates the extent of real choice open to the authorities of former communist countries starting out on reform.[3] Strong-arm regimes may have a degree of choice in the sense that they can use coercive methods when faced with the ill-effects of either reform or failure to reform; but for newly democratic governments – usually quite fragile – there is actually very little room for manoeuvre. There is a window and it is a question of taking this opportunity. However, given rational expectations, people are more likely to believe reforms are on their way if they are global rather than incremental and easily modifiable as soon as unemployment starts to rise and other social ills begin to be felt. When a country has strong aspirations to become a democracy and a market economy, a sense of pace is important, because expectations are high. To choose the slow road either to reduce inflation or to institute reforms means that aspects of the old system remain, thereby sometimes making the task more difficult. This has been illustrated very clearly by the Russian experience – though Russian 'gradualism' has been the result of political obstacles to reform, rather than the conscious policy of the President and government. To quote Gaidar:

> We began the reforms in a very interesting situation when you could have listed many absent preconditions, making reforms impossible to implement at the time. I myself could have given a perfect explanation of why in 1992 the reforms should not have been launched. There was no stable support in the parliament; there were no normal functioning institutions of governance (the army, customs, the police) – they were still staggering from the crisis of power that had begun in the early 1990s.
>
> There were sixteen central banks instead of one; there were no traditions of private enterprise; there was no strong private sector as in Poland. There wasn't a kopeck to be had of hard currency or gold reserves, nor the opportunity to attract free investment from the international financial market. But aside from all that, we couldn't wait any longer. We couldn't just keep doing nothing, or keep explaining why it was impossible to do anything.[4]

The onset of reform does not immediately achieve the goal of providing consumers with choice; but it does give them a set of opportunities. If suddenly they are faced with the choice between the bread queue (i.e. non-reform) and the unemployment queue (i.e. reform), they may choose the unemployment one hoping that one day they will leave it with a real chance of betterment unimaginable in the old system. Few could be expected to prefer unemployment out of a wide range of other options: but such alternative possibilities may not exist – which is not to say that demagogic politicians cannot profit from convincing people that more attractive alternatives are in fact available.

It is important not to confuse the prospective benefits of reform and of stabilization with the real dislocations that characterize the transition from high inflation to price stability (Vegh, 1992, p. 638). The problem is exacerbated in part because the data are obscure. But in any case, to blame the reforms for the output decline is precisely to perpetuate the aforementioned confusions. Actually, the decline in output had started in centrally planned economies before reforms were introduced (Borensztein et al., 1993). It is true that during the early stages of transition, neither the length

Table 6.1. Industrial production in Eastern and Central Europe, 1990–92

Change in percentage	1990	1991	1992	Cumulative change 1990–92
Poland	−26.10%	−11.90%	3.90%	32.35%
Bulgaria	−12.60%	−23.30%	−15.00%	43.01%
Czechoslovakia	−3.50%	−21.20%	−10.60%	32.01%
Hungary	−4.50%	−19.10%	−9.80%	30.31%
Romania	−19.00%	−22.70%	−22.00%	51.16%
Russia	−2.60%	−8.00%	−19.00%	27.41%

Sources: United Nations, Economic Commission for Europe, *Economic Bulletin for Europe*, 1992; IMF (1993a) for Russia.

nor the depth of the fall in production was expected (Calvo and Kumar, 1994). But this phenomenon is not unique to the FSU; on the contrary, the fall in output (approximated by industrial production) occurred in all Eastern and Central European countries, whether they pursued a radical or a gradual policy (Sachs, 1993, p. 6) (Table 6.1). Unfortunately there exist today few studies attempting to quantify the relative impact on output declines of the various possible causes (Williamson, 1992b), and this should be on the agenda for further research, at least when the number of statistical observations becomes sufficient to produce significant results.

We saw in the previous chapters that tight monetary policy was not the cause of output decline in Russia. While the estimated decline in output was large (12.9% in 1991, 19% in 1992 and 12.5% in 1993), changes in employment appeared very small, with registered unemployment remaining in the range of 1.5%–2% of the labour force (Yemtsov, 1994, p. 1) (Table 6.2).

Russia's low unemployment rate is explained by two factors. First, actual unemployment in Russia is both above the recorded unemployment and increasing. The discrepancy between actual and recorded unemployment is due to definition problems. The second factor is more crucial: unemployment remains low because the inflationary credits and subsidies given to state enterprises have supported what is, in effect, disguised unemployment. Low unemployment was preserved in part at the cost of high inflation and in part at the expense of industrial progress and reform itself. As long as enterprises

Table 6.2. Unemployment in Russia, 1992–4 (March/April)

	1992	1993	1994[a]
Registered unemployed[b]	1.1%	1.4%	2.1%
VCIOM survey[c]		6.2%	6.7%
Labour force survey	4.8%	5.5%	5.9%

[a] The 1994 figure for Russia is for the end of April.
[b] Registered as out of work at the Federal Employment Service.
[c] VCIOM estimates for June 1993 are 6.2% against 6.7% in April 1994; these are higher than the Labour Force Survey estimate mainly because they considered the unemployed to be those without primary work or not working at home (Commander and Yemtsov, 1994, p. 10).
Source: Commander and Yemtsov (1994), Table 1, p. 31.

are spared real financial discipline, there is little prospect of the emergence of growth and a low inflation rate. As we have seen, subsidies to firms remained huge in 1992 and even in 1993. Obviously these subsidies were not used to promote viable output but rather to maintain employment, the firm playing the same social security role as in the Soviet system. Given that since late 1993 subsidies to firms, especially in the form of credits from the CBR, have been considerably reduced, it will be interesting to see if, as a result, unemployment starts to pick up in 1995, especially as directed credits to enterprises have been eliminated. Commander and Yemtsov (1994) see signs of an upward shift in unemployment as the composition of the unemployed is becoming less biased towards women. This strongly suggests that the traditional industrial enterprises are starting to face financial difficulties.

Even while the outcome in 1995 of the latest attempt at stabilization remains uncertain, there can be no doubt that the reforms which began with Gaidar's price liberalization in January 1992, and continued with Chubais' mass privatization (which is beyond the scope of this macroeconomic study) have led to the emergence of a genuine market economy (Aslund, 1995), albeit with distinctive distortions and flaws largely conditioned by the uniquely burdensome Soviet inheritance. This has been, in every sense, a very Russian success story.

APPENDIX I: STATISTICAL BACKGROUND

Table A.1. Annual average rate of growth of net material product, USSR[a]

Date	NMP
1951–5	11.3
1956–60	9.1
1961–5	6.4
1966–70	7.7
1971–5	5.6
1976–80	4.3
1981–5	3.6
1986–90	3.2

[a] Net material product (NMP) is equal to net domestic product (NDP) less the net value added to the non-material service sector. Basically most housing, education, cultural activities, health care, tourism and recreation are not included in the NMP accounts. IMF et al. (1990, pp. 3–4) report that 'Officially measured growth of net material product (NMP) averaged some 2 percent in 1986–87, below the average rate reported for the first half of the 1980s. Allowing for hidden inflation (price increases not included in the official price index because they are supposedly offset by quality improvements), output may well have stagnated.'
Source: Narkhoz (various years), quoted in Smith (1993), Table 2.1, p. 30.

Table A.2. Russia: Monetary base, money supply in roubles, monthly inflation rates, M2 velocity and money multiplier, 1991–4

Months	MB (Rbn)[a]	% change	CPI[b]	Rb M2[c]	% change	k= M2/MB[d]	GDP (Rbn)[e]	V= GDP/M2[f]
1991								
December	353		12	998			104	1.3
1992								
January	368	4.2	296	1,011	1.3	2.7	538	6.4
February	396	7.6	27	1,214	20.1	3.1	677	6.7
March	556	40.4	16	1,314	8.2	2.4	822	7.5
April	686	23.4	17	1,477.6	12.5	2.2	997	8.1
May	857	24.9	11	1,546	4.6	1.8	1,039	8.1
June	1,160	35.4	14	1,931	24.9	1.7	1,137	7.1
July	1,437	23.9	7	2,650	37.2	1.8	1,419	6.4
August	2,078	44.6	9	3,322	25.4	1.6	1,388	5.0
September	2,563	23.3	13	4,218	27.0	1.6	1,706	4.9
October	3,211	25.3	31	5,277	25.1	1.6	1,880	4.3
November	3,120	−2.8	27	5,671	7.5	1.8	2,409	5.1
December	4,284.5	37.3	25	6,050	6.7	1.4	2,988	5.9
1993								
January	4,566.6	6.6	26	7,187	18.8	1.6	4,334	7.2
February	5,155.4	12.9	25	7,782	8.3	1.5	5,320	8.2
March	6,344.4	23.1	20	8,913	14.5	1.4	6,147	8.3
April	7,207.4	13.6	19	11,063	24.1	1.5	8,470	9.2
May	8,244.8	14.4	18	13,460	21.7	1.6	9,393	8.4
June	9,403.9	14.1	20	15,765	17.1	1.7	12,149	9.2
July	12,382.1	31.7	22	18,428	16.9	1.5	13,540	8.8
August	13,853	11.9	26	21,121	14.6	1.5	13,571	7.7
September	14,884.3	7.4	23	21,771	3.1	1.5	17,029	9.4
October	16,950.2	13.9	20	24,554	12.8	1.4	19,330	9.4
November	19,014	12.2	16.5	26,788	9.1	1.4	22,704	10.2
December	22,442	18.0	12.5	31,800	18.7	1.4	30,357	11.5
1994								
January	21,400	−4.6	17.9	33,351	4.9	1.6	26,000	9.4
February	24,201	13.1	10.7	35,782	7.3	1.5	32,000	10.7
March	27,058	11.8	7.4	38,823	8.5	1.4	36,200	11.2
April	31,294	15.7	8.5	45,912	18.3	1.5	46,300	12.1
May	34,161	9.2	6.9	51,703	12.6	1.5	47,000	10.9

Continued overleaf

Table A.2. *continued*

Months	MB (Rbn)[a]	% change	CPI[b]	Rb M2[c]	% change	k= M2/MB[d]	GDP (Rbn)[e]	V= GDP/M2[f]
June	38,106	11.5	6.0	58,496	13.1	1.5	48,000	9.8
July	43,114	13.1	5.3	63,297	8.2	1.5	50,000	9.5
August	46,692	8.3	4.6	69,378	9.6	1.5	56,000	9.7
September	50,001	7.1	7.7	74,820	7.8	1.5	61,600	9.9
October	50,407	0.8	11.8	81,452	8.9	1.6	64,600	9.5
November	53,454	6.0	14.2	88,190	8.3	1.6	75,200	10.2
December			16.4				87,100	

[a] Monetary base.

[b] The CPI is the urban index for 1992 (see Koen, 1994, p. 4).

[c] M2 is defined as currency outside banks plus rouble deposits (demand deposits plus time and saving deposits).

[d] k is the money multiplier calculated as M2/MB.

[e] The GDP for 1992 is not the latest estimate; it was revised many times and the only reason for keeping this estimate, which sums to R17,000 billion instead of R18,064 billion, is that it provides the monthly series; the other series is only quarterly.

[f] V is the rouble M2 velocity calculated as the yearly average GDP divided by rouble M2.

Source: *Quarterly Bulletin* of the CBR; author's calculations.

Table A.3. Refinance rate changes, 1992–4

Period	Annual rate (%)
Before 10 April 1992	20
10 April–28 May 1992	50
29 May 1992–29 March 1993	80
30 March–1 June 1993	100
2 June–21 June 1993	110
22 June–28 June 1993	120
29 June–14 July 1993	140
15 July–22 September 1993	170
23 September–14 October 1993	180
15 October1993–28 April 1994	210
29 April–17 May 1994	205
18 May–31 May, 1994	200
1 June–22 June 1994	185
23 June–1 July 1994	170
2 July–22 August 1994	155
23 August 1994	130
12 October 1994	170
17 November 1994	180
6 January 1995	200

Source: CBR.

Table A.4. Russia, total reserves, 1992–3, end of period (Rbn)

	Rouble depostis (RD)	Minimum reserves (MR)	Excess reserves (ER)	Total reserves (TR)[a]	MR/RD (%)	ER/RD (%)	TR/RD (%)
1991							
December	831	8	171	179	1.0	20.6	21.5
1992							
January	827	12	165	177	1.5	20.0	21.4
February	1,007	35.4	147	182.4	3.5	14.6	18.1
March	1,075	86	220	306	8.0	20.5	28.5
April	1,131	91.7	316	407.7	8.1	27.9	36.0
May	1,189	94	398	492	7.9	33.5	41.4
June	1,488	113.5	592	705.5	7.6	39.8	47.4
July	1,951	147	648	795	7.5	33.2	40.7
August	2,592	185	1,091	1,276	7.1	42.1	49.2
September	3,516	254	1,380	1,634	7.2	39.2	46.5
October	4,526	345.8	1,739	2,084.8	7.6	38.4	46.1
November	4,589	420.8	1,345	1,765.8	9.2	29.3	38.5
December	4,371.6	472.4	2,049.5	2,521.9	10.8	46.9	57.7
1993							
January	5,284.5	569.3	1,968.4	2,537.7	10.8	37.2	48.0
February	5,503.4	639.1	2,077.4	2,716.5	11.6	37.7	49.4
March	6,354	730.8	2,790.4	3,521.2	11.5	43.9	55.4
April	7,754.3	891.2	2,762.4	3,653.6	11.5	35.6	47.1
May	9,440.4	1,067.4	2,819.8	3,887.2	11.3	29.9	41.2
June	10,652.3	1,227.1	2,716.9	3,944	11.5	25.5	37.0
July	12,167.1	1,388.8	4,412.1	5,800.9	11.4	36.3	47.7
August	13,814.1	1,615.1	4,407	6,022.1	11.7	31.9	43.6
September	13,362.3	1,894.9	4,114.3	6,009.2	14.2	30.8	45.0
October	14,728.4	2,144.8	4,478.2	6,623	14.6	30.4	45.0
November	15,836.1	2,426.5	4,934	7,360.5	15.3	31.2	46.5
December	18,496	2,709.6	5,751	8,460.6	14.6	31.1	45.7
1994							
January	20,383	3,145	4,390	7,535	15.4	21.5	37.0
February	21,209	3,303	5,460	8,763	15.6	25.7	41.3
March	22,883	3,603	6,626	10,229	15.7	29.0	44.7
April	26,501	4,027	7,002	11,029	15.2	26.4	41.6
May	31,034	4,599	7,692	12,291	14.8	24.8	39.6
June	34,685	5,431	7,748	13,179	15.7	22.3	38.0
July	36,249	6,290	8,436	14,726	17.4	23.3	40.6
August	41,459	7,071	10,067	17,138	17.1	24.3	41.3
September	44,804	8,119	10,139	18,258	18.1	22.6	40.8
October	50,930	8,765	9,127	17,892	17.2	17.9	35.1
November	56,208		10,100			18.0	

[a] TR= total reserves = minimum reserves + excess reserves (correspondent accounts).

Source: *Quarterly Bulletin* of the CBR; author's calculations.

Table A.5. Demand and time deposits in the Sberbank, end of period (Rbn)

	Demand deposits in Sberbank	Time deposits in Sberbank	Total
1992			
January	205.8	172	377.8
February	218.8	176.6	395.4
March	235.9	166.5	402.4
April	247	160	407
May	258.6	156.5	415.1
June	277.5	154.1	431.6
July	293.3	154	447.3
August	307.3	153.5	460.8
September	324.4	153.5	477.9
October	344	155.2	499.2
November	373.7	157.1	530.8
December	440.3	218	658.3
1993			
January	510.4	195.1	705.5
February	585.9	213	798.9
March	572.3	347.7	920
April	615.9	430.9	1,046.8
May	644.2	558.1	1,202.3
June	814.4	584.7	1,399.1
July	920.7	685.8	1,606.5
August	1,035	799.7	1,834.7
September	1,123.3	891.8	2,015.1
October	1,226.3	1,044.7	2,271
November	1,371.6	1,256.1	2,627.7
December	1,850.9	2,115.9	3,966.8
1994			
January	1,948.1	2,278.6	4,226.7
February	2,094.9	2,584.6	4,679.5
March	2,226.8	2,941.6	5,168.4
April	2,346.5	3,307.6	5,654.1
May	2,573	3,859.4	6,432.4
June	2,578.7	5,204.2	7,782.9
July	2,901.2	5,890.2	8,791.4
August	3,063.8	7,148.8	10,212.6
September			11,773.3
October			12,399.2
November			13,671.4

Source: CBR.

Table A.6. Foreign exchange deposits, rouble deposits and broad money, end of period (Rbn).

	Currency outside banks	Rouble deposits	Foreign exchange deposits	Broad money[a]	Rouble M2[b]
December 1991	167	831	203	1,201	998
1992					
January	183.8	827.2	241	1,252	1,011
February	209.3	1,005	279	1,493	1,214
March	247.6	1,066	319	1,633	1,314
April	317.5	1,160	376	1,854	1,477.6
May	365.6	1,180	598	2,144	1,546
June	455.1	1,476	852	2,783	1,931
July	643	2,007	1,132	3,782	2,650
August	804	2,518	1,566	4,888	3,322
September	950	3,268	2,534	6,752	4,218
October	1,146	4,131	4,100	9,377	5,277
November	1,380	4,291	4,749	10,420	5,671
December	1,678.4	4,372	4,538	10,588	6,050
1993					
January	1,902.5	5,285	6,227	13,414	7,187
February	2,278.6	5,503	6,539	14,321	7,782
March	2,559	6,354	7,671	16,584	8,913
April	3,308.7	7,754	9,353	20,416	11,063
May	4,019.6	9,440	11,824	25,284	13,460
June	5,112.7	10,652	12,053	27,818	15,765
July	6,260.9	12,167	9,123	27,551	18,428
August	7,306.9	13,814	8,341	29,462	21,121
September	8,408.7	13,362	11,421	33,192	21,771
October	9,825.6	14,728	12,473	37,027	24,554
November	10,952	15,836	13,532	40,320	26,788
December	13,304	18,496	14,080	45,880	31,800
1994					
January	12,968	20,383	18,666	52,017	33,351
February	14,573	21,209	20,245	56,027	35,782
March	15,940	22,883	21,637	60,460	38,823
April	19,411	26,501	21,930	67,842	45,912
May	20,669	31,034	22,157	73,860	51,703
June	23,811	34,685	21,952	80,448	58,496

[a] Broad money is calculated as currency outside banks + rouble deposits + foreign exchange deposits.
[b] Rouble M2 is calculated as currency outside banks + rouble deposits.
Source: CBR data.

Table A.7. Seigniorage

	Rouble currency (Rbn)	MB1 (Rbn)	MB2 (Rbn)	SEC (%)	SE1 (%)	SE2 (%)
December 1991	167	353	182			
1992						
January	183.8	368	203	3.1	2.8	3.9
February	209.3	396	249	3.8	4.1	6.8
March	247.6	556	336	4.7	19.5	10.6
April	317.5	686	370	7.0	13.0	3.4
May	365.6	857	459	4.6	16.5	8.6
June	455.1	1,160	568	7.9	26.6	9.6
July	643	1,437	789	13.2	19.5	15.6
August	804	2,078	987	11.6	46.2	14.3
September	950	2,563	1,183	8.6	28.4	11.5
October	1,146	3,211	1,472	10.4	34.5	15.4
November	1,380	3,120	1,775	9.7	−3.8	12.6
December	1,678.4	4,284.5	2,235	10.0	39.0	15.4
1993						
January	1,902.5	4,566.6	2,598.2	5.2	6.5	8.4
February	2,278.6	5,155.4	3,078	7.1	11.1	9.0
March	2,559	6,344.4	3,554	4.6	19.3	7.7
April	3,308.7	7,207.4	4,445	8.9	10.2	10.5
May	4,019.6	8,244.8	5,425	7.6	11.0	10.4
June	5,112.7	9,403.9	6,687	9.0	9.5	10.4
July	6,260.9	12,382.1	7,970	8.5	22.0	9.5
August	7,306.9	13,853	9,446	7.7	10.8	10.9
September	8,408.7	14,884.3	10,770	6.5	6.1	7.8
October	9,825.6	16,950.2	12,472	7.3	10.7	8.8
November	10,951.9	19,014	14,080	5.0	9.1	7.1
December	13,304	22,442	16,691	7.7	11.3	8.6
1994						
January	12,968	21,400	17,010	−1.3	−4.0	1.2
February	14,573	24,201	18,741	5.0	8.8	5.4
March	15,940	27,058	20,432	3.8	7.9	4.7
April	19,411	31,294	24,292	7.5	9.1	8.3
May	20,669	34,161	26,469	2.7	6.1	4.6
June	23,811	38,106	30,358	6.5	8.2	8.1
July	27,048	43,114	34,678	6.5	10.0	8.6
August	27,919	46,692	36,625	1.6	6.4	3.5

Continued overleaf

Table A.7. *continued*

	Rouble currency (Rbn)	MB1 (Rbn)	MB2 (Rbn)	SEC (%)	SE1 (%)	SE2 (%)
September	30,016	50,001	39,862	3.4	5.4	5.3
October	30,522	50,407	41,280	0.8	0.6	2.2
November	31,982	53,454	43,354	1.9	4.1	2.8

MB1: Monetary base including excess reserves.
MB2: Monetary base excluding excess reserves.
SEC: Seigniorage on rouble currency.
SE1: Seigniorage on the monetary base (including excess reserves).
SE2: Seigniorage on the monetary base (excluding excess reserves).
Source: Goskomstat; CBR; author's calulations.

Table A.8. Average nominal and real wages, end of period

	Nominal wage		Real wage[a]	
	% change	R/mth	% change	w/p
1992				
January		1,438		100
February	39	2,004	9	109.47
March	36	2,726	17	127.93
April	11	3,024	−5	121.09
May	21	3,672	10	133.07
June	38	5,067	21	161.21
July	8	5,452	0	161.96
August	8	5,870	−1	160.57
September	26	7,379	9	175.22
October	20	8,853	−8	160.35
November	19	10,576	−6	150.71
December[b]	52	16,071	21	182.78
1993				
January	−2	15,690	−22	141.85
February	19	18,672	−5	135.37
March	26	23,559	5	142.21
April	30	30,562	9	155.29
May	23	37,505	4	161.36
June	26	47,371	5	169.99
July	18	55,995	−3	164.16
August	17	65,408	−7	152.19
September	24	80,900	1	153.04
October	15	93,000	−4	147.22
November	9	101,500	−6	137.92
December[b]	39	141,283	24	170.64
1994				
January	−5	134,200	−19	137.48
February	8	144,700	−3	133.91
March	14	164,800	6	142.00
April	4	171,400	−4	136.12
May	7	183,500	0	136.32
June	13	207,500	7	145.42
July	7	221,000	1	147.09
August	5	232,800	1	148.13
September	9	253,200	1	149.59
October	5	265,000	−6	140.04
November	6	281,600	−7	130.31
December[b]	26	354,200	8	140.81

[a] w/p is the real wage calculated as the average nominal wage deflated by the CPI.
[b] The jump in December is due to the fact that a 13th month is paid.
Source: Goskomstat.

Table A.9. Nominal and real interest rates and inflation, end of period (%)

	Refinance rate[a]	Effective yield	Monthly rate[b]	Inflation (monthly)[c]	Real refinance rate (monthly)
1992					
January	20.0	21.9	1.7	296.0	−74.3
February	20.0	21.9	1.7	27.3	−20.1
March	20.0	21.9	1.7	16.4	−12.7
April	50.0	63.2	4.2	17.2	−11.1
May	80.0	116.9	6.7	10.5	−3.5
June	80.0	116.9	6.7	13.9	−6.4
July	80.0	116.9	6.7	7.1	−0.4
August	80.0	116.9	6.7	8.6	−1.8
September	80.0	116.9	6.7	13.2	−5.8
October	80.0	116.9	6.7	31.1	−18.6
November	80.0	116.9	6.7	27.1	−16.1
December	80.0	116.9	6.7	25.3	−14.9
1993					
January	80.0	116.9	6.7	26	−15.2
February	80.0	116.9	6.7	25	−14.5
March	80.0	116.9	6.7	20	−11.2
April	100.0	161.3	8.3	19	−8.8
May	100.0	161.3	8.3	18	−8.3
June	140.0	275.9	11.7	20	−6.9
July	170.0	390.3	14.2	22.4	−6.7
August	170.0	390.3	14.2	26.0	−9.4
September	180.0	435.0	15.0	23.0	−6.5
October	210.0	592.6	17.5	19.5	−1.7
November	210.0	592.6	17.5	16.5	0.9
December	210.0	592.6	17.5	12.5	4.4
1994					
Janaury	210.0	592.6	17.5	17.9	−0.3
February	210.0	592.6	17.5	10.7	6.1
March	210.0	592.6	17.5	7.4	9.4
April	210.0	592.6	17.5	8.5	8.3
May	202.5	549.6	16.9	6.9	9.3
June	177.5	423.5	14.8	6.0	8.3
July	155.0	329.6	12.9	5.3	7.2
August	142.5	284.4	11.9	4.6	7.0

Continued

Table A.9. *continued*

	Refinance rate[a]	Effective yield	Monthly rate[b]	Inflation (monthly)[c]	Real refinance rate (monthly)
September	130.0	243.6	10.8	7.7	2.9
October	150.0	311.0	12.5	11.8	0.6
November	175.0	412.2	14.6	14.2	0.3
December	180.0	435.0	15.0	16.4	−1.2
January 1995	200.0	535.9	16.7	17.8	−1.0

[a] The overdraft refinance rate is twice the refinance rate; so, for example, if in September 1993 the refinance rate was 180%, the overdraft refinance rate was 360%.

[b] The real interest rate is $R = [(1+n/12)/(1+\pi)]-1$

[c] The urban price index is used for 1992, the expanded one thereafter. Yearly inflation is defined as $(1+\pi)^{12}-1$.

Source: CBR, *Yearly Report* and various monthly reports.

Table A.10. Real interest rate on credits and deposits, end of period (%)

	Deposit rate, monthly	Real deposit rate, monthly	Credit rate, monthly	Real credit rate, monthly
1992				
January	1.2			
February	1.6	−20.2		
March	2.1	−12.3	3.8	−10.8
April	3.3	−11.9		
May	3.7	−6.1		
June	4.7	−8.1	7.4	−5.7
July	4.9	−2.0		
August	5.6	−2.8		
September	5.6	−8.3	9.0	−5.4
October	6.0	−19.2		
November	6.2	−16.4		
December	6.5	−14.9	10.1	−12.0
1993				
January	6.4	−15.4	10.6	−12.1
February	6.8	−14.4	11.0	−11.0
March	7.5	−10.5	12.1	−6.7
April	8.3	−8.8	12.4	−5.4
May	8.7	−8.0	12.9	−4.4
June	9.5	−8.7	13.3	−5.5
July	10.3	−9.9	14.1	−6.8
August	10.8	−12.1	15.4	−8.4
September	11.1	−9.7	16.2	−5.5
October	12.2	−6.1	17.0	−2.1
November	12.3	−3.6	17.5	0.9
December	12.6	0.1	18.1	5.0
1994				
January	13.3	−3.9	18.1	0.2
February	13.5	2.5	18.4	7.0
March	13.7	5.9	18.7	10.5
April	13.4	4.5	18.5	9.2
May	12.1	4.9	17.1	9.5
June	9.9	3.7	16.1	9.5
July	9.6	4.1	14.1	8.4
August	8.3	3.5	13.0	8.0
September	6.9	−0.7	12.0	4.0

Note: *r* is the real interest rate and is calculated as: $r = \dfrac{1 + n/12}{1 + \pi} - 1$

Source: *Russian Economic Trends*, 1993, vol. 2, no. 3; 1994, vol. 3, no. 1; author's calculations.

Table A.11. Russia: credit and inter-enterprise arrears, 1992, end of period

	Commercial banks' rouble credit to enterprises (Rbn)	Real bank credit[a] (Rbn)	Nominal arrears (Rbn)	Real arrears[a] (Rbn)	Nominal arrears/ bank (%)	IEA/GDP (%)	Bank credit/ GDP (%)
1991							
December	594		34.0		6		
1992							
January	606	606.0	140.5	140	23		
February	833	603.6	605.8	439	73		
March	1,010	628.8	744.5	463	74	41	55
April	1,208	641.7	1,855	985	154		
May	1,232	592.2	2,057	989	167		
June	1,645	694.3	3,004	1,268	183	66	28
July[b]	2,332	919.0	1,876	739	80		
August	2,841	1,030.9	1,084	393	38		
September	3,606	1,135.8	440.2	139	12	5	38
October	4,663	1,120.3	397.4	95	9		
November	5,461	1,032.3	521.3	99	10		
December	5,982	903.9	598	90	10	3	33

[a] Real bank credits and real arrears are calculated as the nominal bank credits and the nominal arrears deflated by the CPI.

[b] The sharp decline in July 1992 is due to the netting out which took place at the time.

Source: CBR; author's calculations.

Table A.12. Overdue cash payments to individuals, 1992, end of period (Rbn)

	Mar.	Apr.	May	June	July	Aug.	Sep.	Oct.	Nov.	Dec.
Total	31.8	78.5	149.9	221.6	114					
Delayed wage payments in industry, construction and agriculture	14.6	22.2	54.4	65.1	47.6	28.2	21.5	29.9	33.6	28.8
of which: Owing to shortage of cash in banks	9.6	13.1	38.4	46.4	28.7	7.9	2.8	2.5	1.3	0.6
Overdue social allowance and wage payments in sectors other than industry, agriculture and construction	17.2	56.3	95.5	156.5	66.4					
Owing to shortage of cash in banks (for all payments)	26.7	69.4	134	202.9						

Source: Koen and Phillips (1993, Table 12, p. 45).

Table A.13. Moscow currency-exchange market: volume of transactions, exchange rate and CBR interventions

Date	Exchange rate end of period (R/US$)	Exchange rate average (R/US$)	Monthly volume of transactions in US$m	CBR intervention[a] in US$ m
January 1992	230	213.4	18	
February	139	186	33	
March	160.4	150.2	99	
April	143.6	154	47	
May	113	120.5	100	
June	144	126	308.92	
July	161.2	143	253.57	
August	210.5	168	261.3	
September	309	220	453.1	
October	398	354	408.9	
November	417	426	353.2	
December	414.5	415	453	−102.00
January 1993	572	484	485.1	154.60
February	593	569	518.6	185.00
March	684	665	494.9	122.10
April	823	767	576.8	244.00
May	1024	928	437.13	197.20
June	1060	1080	676.8	−101.50
July	987	1025	1361.7	−923.40
August	992.5	986	1236.9	447.10
September	1169	1072	2190.1	1005.20
October	1184	1187.7	1244.9	4.00
November	1231	1194.5	1616.3	425.10
December	1247	1240.3	1848.9	−143.40
January 1994	1548	1444.4	2094.8	1053.10
February	1659	1583.3	1696.8	180.70
March	1753	1718.68	1279.05	123.10
April	1832	1793.7	1157.9	−60.40
May	1916	1881.7	1112.8	267.30
June	1989	1959.2	1395.6	
July	2060	2025.9	1456.75	
August	2197	2121.7	3802.85	
September	2633	2346.9	3569.7	
October	3075	3043.5	2550.27	
November	3234	3151.4	1502.92	
December	3550	3387.7	1673.01	

[a] Central Bank of Russia net sales/purchases at MICEX.

Source: Author's calculations; MICEX; and CBR interventions from IMF (1995), Table 59, p. 122.

Table A.14. Adjusted interest–rate differential, end of period

	Interbank lending rate on 1–3 month credit[a]	Yields annual	Yields monthly i	Foreign interest rate[b] $(a)if$	Exchange rate e	Depreciation/ appreciation de/e	Adjusted interest differential[c] $i–if–de/e$
1992							
January	26.6	30	2.22	0.5	230		
February	33.3	39	2.78	0.5	139	−39.6	41.8
March	38.8	47	3.23	0.5	160.4	15.4	−12.7
April	46.9	58	3.91	0.5	143.6	−10.5	13.9
May	68.7	95	5.73	0.5	113	−21.3	26.5
June	81.0	119	6.75	0.5	144	27.4	−21.2
July	92.3	143	7.69	0.5	161.2	11.9	−4.8
August	98.8	158	8.23	0.5	210.5	30.6	−22.8
September	99.3	160	8.28	0.5	309	46.8	−39.0
October	103.0	169	8.58	0.5	398	28.8	−20.7
November	106.9	178	8.91	0.5	417	4.8	3.6
December	114.6	199	9.55	0.5	414.5	−0.6	9.6
1993							
January	118.8	210	9.9	0.50	572	38.0	−28.6
February	128.8	240	10.73	0.5	593	3.7	6.6
March	132.1	250	11.01	0.5	684	15.3	−4.8
April	135.2	260	11.27	0.5	823	20.3	−9.6
May	140.4	277	11.70	0.5	1,024	24.4	−13.2
June	145.1	293	12.09	0.5	1,060	3.5	8.1
July	174.0	408	14.50	0.5	987	−6.9	20.9
August	185.0	459	15.42	0.5	992.5	0.6	14.4
September	187.6	471	15.63	0.5	1,169	17.8	−2.7
October	201.8	546	16.82	0.5	1,184	1.3	15.0
November	213.6	614	17.80	0.5	1,231.0	4.0	13.3
December	205.6	567	17.14	0.5	1,247	1.3	15.3
1994							
January	214.4	619	17.86	0.5	1,548	24.1	−6.8
February	213.3	612	17.78	0.5	1,659	7.2	10.1
March	210.6	596	17.55	0.5	1,753	5.7	11.4
April	203.4	555	16.95	0.5	1,832	4.5	11.9
May	179.9	435	14.99	0.5	1,916	4.6	9.9
June	147.3	301	12.27	0.5	1,989	3.8	8.0

Continued

Table A.14. *continued*

	Interbank lending rate on 1–3 month credit[a]	Yields annual	Yields monthly i	Foreign interest rate[b] $(a)if$	Exchange rate e	Depreciation/ appreciation de/e	Adjusted interest differential[c] $i-if-de/e$
July	140.4	277	11.70	0.5	2,060	3.6	7.6
August	124.2	226	10.35	0.5	2,204	7.0	2.9
September	119.9	214	9.99	0.5	2,633	19.5	−10.0
October	138.8	272	11.56	0.5	3,075	16.8	−5.7
November	162.9	361	13.57	0.5	3,234	5.2	7.9
December	163.7	364	13.64	0.5	3,550	9.8	3.4

[a] The interbank interest rates are calculated from press reports (average).

[b] Interest rates on foreign-exchange deposits were between 5% and 12% in 1992, so the average rate is assumed to be equal to 0.5% per month.

[c] A negative sign at the front of the adjusted interest differential means that it is more profitable to invest in dollars than in roubles.

Source: MICEX; press reports; author's calculations.

Table A.15. Net international reserves, end of period

	NIR (Rbn)	Net CBR foreign exchange (1)	Net government foreign exchange (2)	Total (US$m) (1) + (2)	Exchange rate (R/US$)
December 1992	1,249.30	1,871	1,143	3,014	414.5
1993					
January	2,072.36	2,009	1,614	3,623	572
February	2,232.05	2,104	1,660	3,764	593
March	2811.24	2,167	1,943	4,110	684
April	3,787.45	2,266	2,336	4,602	823
May	5,329.92	2,781	2,424	5,205	1,024
June	6,407.70	3,355	2,690	6,045	1,060
July	6,865.57	5,122	1,834	6,956	987
August	7,549.95	6,161	1,446	7,607	992.5
September	7,582.13	5,753	733	6,486	1,169
October	7,402.37	5,670	582	6,252	1,184
November	7,786.08	5,398	927	6,325	1,231
December	7,940.90	5,855	513	6,368	1,247
1994					
January	6,645.26	4,545	784	5,329	1,247
February	6,230.01	4,292	704	4,996	1,247
March	6,374.66	4,819	293	5,112	1,247
April	6,671.45	5,414	−64	5,350	1,247
May	6,571.69	5,470	−200	5,270	1,247
June	7,970.82	6,293	99	6,392	1,247
July	7,099.17	6,340	−647	5,693	1,247
August	4,966.80	5,151	−1,168	3,983	1,247
September	3,328.24	4,238	−1,569	2,669	1,247
October	2,503.98	3,523	−1,515	2,008	1,247
November	2,000.19	4,056	−2,452	1,604	1,247

Source: CBR; author's calculations.

Table A.16. Monthly change in M2 (DM2), monthly inflation rate (DP) and monthly change in average nominal exchange rate (DE) (%)

	1992			1993			1994		
	DM2	DP	DE	DM2	DP	DE	DM2	DP	DE
January	1.3	296		18.8	26	16.6	4.9	17.9	16.5
February	20.1	27	−12.8	8.3	25	17.6	7.3	10.7	9.6
March	8.2	16	−19.2	14.5	20	16.8	8.5	7.4	8.6
April	12.5	17	2.5	24.1	19	15.4	18.3	8.5	4.4
May	4.6	11	−21.8	21.7	18	21.0	12.6	6.9	4.9
June	24.9	14	4.6	17.1	20	16.4	13.1	6.0	4.1
July	37.2	7	13.5	16.9	22	−5.1	8.2	5.3	3.4
August	25.4	9	17.5	14.6	26	−3.8	9.6	4.6	4.7
September	27.0	15	31.0	3.1	23	8.7	7.8	7.7	10.6
October	25.1	31	60.9	12.8	20	10.8	8.9	11.8	29.7
November	7.5	27	20.3	9.1	17	0.6	8.3	14.2	3.5
December	6.7	25	−2.6	18.7	13	3.8		16.4	7.5

Source: Goskomstat; CBR; MICEX; author's calculations.

APPENDIX 2: DATA DESCRIPTION

This appendix is designed to explain the data used in this book, and also to explain the inevitability of the occasional lack of precision.

Statistics for Russia vary in quality and availability, but are generally poor by Western standards. I have used the IMF series where possible, although these series also have shortcomings. In the real sector the source of data is the State Committee for Statistics (Goskomstat); in the monetary sector the Central Bank.

Monetary data

There is particular difficulty in compiling monetary statistics for Russia. The problems, well-known to economists working in this field, include the authorities' failure to provide regular updated series of comparable figures (many of which were in 1992 and unfortunately still are in 1995 regarded as classified information).

There exist at present about four different time series for M2, all produced by different departments of the CBR. The IMF recalculates its own series using the balance sheet of the CBR, which is very hard to read. Here the series used is approximately that used in the IMF negotiations (though subject to many revisions). These five different series all differed in methodology. For instance in the IMF methodology preferred here M2 excludes 'government deposits' since they were not submitted to minimum reserve requirement. Foreign-exchange deposits are deposits held by the Russian banking system.

Foreign-exchange reserves

Monthly data on gross CBR reserves, and foreign assets and liabilities of the government are published by the CBR in *Current Tendencies in the Monetary and Credit Sphere*.

Gross domestic product

GDP is published monthly in the Goskomstat report *Ekonomicheskoe Polozhene Rossiskoi Federatsii*. The problem here is that, for instance in 1992, the series was frequently changed. In IMF (1993a) for 1992, GDP is quoted as R15,552 bn, but Goskomstat published a final figure for 1992 of R18064.5 bn. This explains why so many differences can exist between different authors. Much depends on the chosen figure on which calculations are based.

Interest rates

The interest rate is quoted per annum, non-compounded. If the non-compounded rate is i% and the maturity of the deposit or loan contract is one year, the corresponding compounded rate is $[(1+i/(12 \times 100))^{12}-1] \times 100$.

The CBR refinance rate is quoted from the press which reports all changes made by the CBR.

The inter-bank interest rates are calculated from press reports (average) until December 1993. Starting in December 1993 the inter-bank rate given is the average of the weekly rates quoted in *Vestnik Banka Rossi* produced by the CBR every week.

Rates on deposits and credits are from *Russian Economic Trends*.

Prices

Monthly: For the calculations of the time series, the urban CPI is used for 1992 and the expanded CPI for 1993 and 1994. As explained in Koen (1994, p. 3) the urban index was a standard Laspeyres designed in mid-1992. It originally covered 27 urban areas and 262 items; for 1993 and 1994 its coverage was 'expanded' to all oblast centres and 407 items. However, until the end of 1993 Goskomstat quoted the hybrid index as the CPI, and so did the press and literature. The hybrid index was a mixture of Paasche and Laspeyres indices and that is why Koen and Phillips (1993) called it the hybrid CPI. The hybrid and urban index led to substantially different results: for instance, for January 1992 the CPI is either 245% or 296% depending on the index used.

These issues are far from trivial. Detailed descriptions of these indices are given in Koen and Phillips (1993), Koen (1994), Koen and Meyermans (1994) and in Granville and Shapiro (1994).

In December 1994, Goskomstat changed its methodology without notifying anyone or even trying to reconcile the series. The 16.4% figure given for December 1994 is based on weekly indices and is not comparable with the previous figures in the series, which use a monthly index. The actual December 1994 figure was more in the range of 17.6%; however, this information was deemed irrelevant, which means that in the course of 1995 the whole 1994 series will probably be revised again.

Exchange rates

The interbank exchange rate is the rate quoted and published by the Moscow Interbank Currency Exchange (MICEX). It is published five times a week.

Wages

Figures are published by Goskomstat in *Ekonomicheskoe Polozhenoe Rossiskoi Federatsii*. Average monthly wages for Russia are net of benefits. The variations in December and January are not significant because in December traditionally a 13th month is paid.

Unemployment

Russian unemployment statistics, like output statistics (see Gavrilenkov and Koen, 1994), are subject to several biases: the Russian definition excludes all job seekers who have an alternative income, e.g. students, pensioners. Only a small proportion of 'real' job seekers register as unemployed, owing to the small benefits given and the bureaucracy involved in getting such benefits. State enterprises tend to keep workers on their payroll who are in fact on indefinite vacation or who are working substantially reduced hours. Also, some industrial enterprises have been forced into temporary closures, which led to a reduction of total working days by six days for each industrial worker in 1993 (Yemtsov, 1994, p. 2). On the other hand, new employment in the private sector is not well reported.

NOTES

Introduction

1 In a joke of the Brezhnev era, a Soviet boss describes the economic system thus: 'You pretend to work, we pretend to pay you.'

2 According to the constitution approved on 12 December 1993, the chairman of the CBR is now proposed by the President and appointed by the lower chamber of parliament, the State Duma.

3 In a profile of Gerashchenko published in *Izvestiya* on 29 October 1994, Irina Savvateeva asked why, given that in 1992–3 Gerashchenko pumped the centralized credits through his favourite banks, making the 'money trade' the most profitable business in Russia, Chernomyrdin supported him in 1993. The answer she gave was that the Imperial Bank, which held most of Gazprom's funds, was run by Sergei Rodionov, a protégé of Gerashchenko. She further makes the point that in the July 1993 currency reform Gerashchenko concluded agreements with various former Soviet Republics on exchanging the old banknotes after the expiry of the official deadlines: again their business was channelled through his favourite commercial banks, making them hundreds of millions of dollars.

4 Speech delivered at the Conference on Finance and Monetary Policy in Russia (*Ekonomika i Zhizn'*, 1993, no. 50), quoted in Popov (1994), p. 11.

5 For details see Granville and Shapiro (1994).

Chapter 1: The political and economic legacy

1 Quoted in Nuti (1986), p. 51.

2 The former Czechoslovakia was formally renamed the Czech and Slovak Federal Republic in April 1990 under pressure from the Slovaks who had wanted their own republic since 1969. Indeed the 1918 Pittsburgh Agreement established the 'Czecho-Slovak Republic.' On 1 January 1993, the country divided into two separate states.

3 Calculated with rouble M2 equal to R998 bn at the end of 1991 (Appendix

1, Table A.2) and with a GDP for 1991 of R1,300 bn (Table 1.3).

4 This debt amounted to about 9% of GDP at the official exchange rate of R1.7:US$1, or 566% of GDP at the commercial exchange rate which at the end of December was R108:US$1.

5 'Only US$60 million which was equal to about 10 hours of imports' (Schneider, 1994, p. 6).

6 According to the 1977 constitution, the 15 union republics had the right to secede and to enter into relations with foreign states. By December 1990, all 15 republics had declared their independence or the sovereignty of their laws over those of the Union. Throughout 1991, efforts were made to develop a new basis for interrepublican relations.

7 As pointed out by the IMF (1993, p. 8), this refers to the 'notional' budget deficit, defined as follows on p. 59 of the same report: 'The "notional" deficit for 1991 refers to the actual outcome of the fiscal operations of the Russian general government, including the takeover of fiscal responsibilities of the former union government, together with the imputed revenues and expenditures that would have been effected by the Russian government had the takeover of union functions agreed to for November–December 1991 actually covered all of 1991.'

8 The *Moscow Times* (Friday 23 September 1994) was running the following story written by Margaret Shapiro of the *Washington Post*: 'Today Pavlov has left coups and communism behind. He is a banker who shuns affiliation with any party, bemoans bureaucratic and mafia meddling in business, drives an Audi, eats at restaurants catering to Moscow's new rich and has a two-story brick country house in one of the nicest spots outside Moscow ... Today his concerns are no longer "building socialism in one country" as the old Soviet slogan had it, but "building a market in one individual family". Pavlov, wearing a watch with diamonds on it, laughed heartily when he said this. His son is also a banker in Luxembourg. His wife is the financial director of a local business ... Pavlov said he does not miss politics at all. He has no intention of joining any political party and thinks that none of them – including his old allies, the communists – have come up with a programme to solve the country's problems. His major personal gripe is all the time he wasted before becoming a businessman, first as Soviet finance and prime minister and then in prison awaiting trial for his involvement in the August 1991 coup. "I lost a year and a half before August and a year and a half after", he said. "If I'd been engaged in my own affairs instead of the government, I'd probably be among the richest men in the country today." '

9 Assuming real output constant, the inflation tax is defined as being equal to πm, where π is the inflation rate and m is the real money base. So the real money base is the tax base and the rate of inflation is the tax rate.

10 'Monetary breakdown' is here meant in the sense of unsustainable repressed inflation.

Chapter 2: Price liberalization

1 For details see Yeltsin (1994), p. 167.

2 The figure of 382% is calculated using a Sauerbeck price index (see Lequiller and Zieschang, 1994). The urban price change was 296% while the so-called hybrid consumer price index was 245%. See Koen and Phillips (1993), Koen (1994) and Appendix 2.

3 Also, because people expected further liberalization of prices and thus higher prices, the demand to hold inventories in January–February 1992 was high. This can be explained both by lack of belief in the reform programme and, probably to a greater degree, by habit, certainly at the consumer level. Already in December 1991, people were stocking up considerably in anticipation of inflation. But in January–February 1992 such stocks became a new sort of holding, piled up not only in anticipation of further price increases, but also as an instinctive response to the appearance on the market of goods which people had become accustomed to think of as naturally in shortage. As far as enterprises were concerned, stockpiling was carried out mainly in anticipation of higher prices.

4 These figures are taken from a study carried out by the author for the Delegation of the EC Commission in Moscow during the first month of price liberalization.

5 The 'energy price' is a weighted average of oil, coal and gas, the weights equalling the respective shares in total energy consumption.

6 In Berg et al. (1993) the monthly inflation index (DCPI) is regressed on a three-month lagged moving average of energy price inflation (DEPR), for all available periods since price liberalization (May 1992 through May 1993):

$$DCPI = 0.190 \quad -0.062*DEPR \qquad R^2 = 0.052$$
$$ (7.58) \quad (-0.78)$$

the t-statistics are in parenthesis. The number of observations is too low for strict interpretation of these t-statistics. All the various possible lag lengths for the energy inflation variable were tried. It was never close to statistical significance.

7   See Delpla (1993) for a detailed study on profit margins. This kind of legislation (decrees of 31 December 1992 and 18 January 1993) aims at curbing inflation by an indirect price cap: a firm cannot sell its products with a profit exceeding x% of its production costs (with 15% < x < 50%).

8   The resolution stated that all companies would have equal access to export facilities but that each potential exporter would need to obtain quarterly export allocations from a joint government commission, which was to include representatives of the Economics Ministry, Fuel and Energy Ministry and the Foreign Trade Ministry. This commission will determine access to Russia's limited export pipeline capacity each quarter according to potential exporters' domestic sales and supplies to the government. The resolution sets no specific percentage of the total oil output companies must sell domestically before striking foreign deals. Instead the government reserves the opportunity to change the domestic sales criteria on a quarterly basis, delegating any dispute settlement to the joint commission. The original June 1994 deadline was extended by six months when the Fuel and Energy Ministry argued that an end to quotas would result in a massive flow of cheap oil abroad and shortages at home.

9   'At the end of 1990, the overhang of unwanted asset holdings for households was estimated to imply a 50% price increase in the event of price liberalisation. At the end of 1991 the "asset overhang" (defined as income rising faster than the supply of consumer goods) of households would have implied a price increase of 143 percent' (World Bank, 1992, p. 13).

Chapter 3: Monetary policy

1   The definitions of the Russian monetary aggregates are as follows: M0: currency in circulation and some cash in vaults; M1: M0 plus the transferable deposits of enterprises and the sight deposits of households with the Sberbank (the savings bank); M2: M1 plus time deposits of households with the savings bank.

2   It might be argued that to take January 1992 as a base is wrong since the jump in prices in that very month substantially lowered the currency's liquidity. However, if December 1991 is taken instead, by August 1992 total real reserves still amounted to 60% of their December 1991 level, not bad considering the high rate of inflation.

3 Khoo and Tsepliaeva (1994) statistically tested all the explanations given in the literature and did not find any statistical significance. They therefore attribute the phenomenon to the slowness of the money creation process.

4 The Moscow Interbank Currency Exchange (MICEX) announced on 22 April 1993 that the first auction of three-month state bonds would take place on 18 May. The government was planning to cover R600 billion of budget deficit through the sale of these bonds; in fact only a third (about R230 billion) of the sum planned was covered. These Treasury bills had a three-month maturity; in December 1993 six-month bonds began to be issued to a value of R10 billion.

5 In Russia, interest rates are quoted on an annual percentage rate (APR) basis rather than on an annual yield (or effective interest) basis. When the compounding basis is monthly, this implies that the annual yield is:
$\gamma = (1+n/12)^{12}-1$, with $\gamma > n$.

In comparing the annual nominal interest rate and the annual inflation rate, the yield and not the APR is the appropriate nominal interest rate. Table A.9 in Appendix 1 shows that if the APR is 180% per annum, the monthly interest rate is $n/12$, i.e. 15%, and the expected annual nominal interest rate is 435%. This is the rate that should be compared with the expected annual inflation rate.

6 In May 1993 the government and the CBR in their agreed 'Economic Policy Statement of the Government of Russia and Central Bank of Russia' committed themselves to cutting the inflation rate to 5% monthly by the end of 1993 (outturn: 12.5%). This agreement was the basis for the negotiations with the IMF of a $3 billion loan under the new Structural Transformation Facility (STF).

7 However, the large increase in the first half of 1993 compared with 1992 is mainly owing to the sharp depreciation of the rouble against the dollar during 1992 and 1993. See Freinkman (1994, p. 4): 'The growth of officially registered enterprise hard currency deposits was 15 times lower in real terms than in 1992.'

8 IMF (1993a, p. 30). These figures varied according to different sources: for example, Ickes and Ryterman (1992, p. 1) give figures of R48 billion in January 1992 and R2.5 trillion by mid-June 1992.

9 GDP for the first six months of 1992 was R4,564.9 (Goskomstat). Rostowski (1993, p. 2) gives the following figures for Poland and the CSFR: 'In the CSFR, IED (inter enterprise debt) constituted about 18% of GDP at the end of 1991, a level to which it had merely doubled from the beginning of the year. In Poland at the end of 1989 IED/GDP ratio

was also around 18% after which it declined.'

10 'The CBR changed the regulations regarding the Kartoteka 2 accounts. Payment demands in most cases were henceforth not to be queued if the recipient firm had insufficient funds to pay the amount due, but were instead to be returned to the originator.' (Fan and Schaffer, 1994, p. 173)

11 For a full description of the system see Sachs and Lipton (1992), p. 12.

12 The VAT rate was later reduced by parliament to 20%. The tax base for VAT is defined as 'cash receipts less cash expenditures for raw materials and other inputs other than wages, with some allowance for depreciation. Receipts and expenditures are officially booked when a soft rouble (bank deposit) payment in settlement of a claim is made through a bank.' (Ickes and Ryterman, 1992, p. 21)

13 This is confirmed by the study of Fishlow and Friedman (1994), which shows that compliance falls when output drops or when expectations about future income improve.

14 'Bankruptcy laws are only a necessary, but far from sufficient, condition for the existence of a bankruptcy system. If courts have no experience of bankruptcy cases and of how to rule on their complexities a high "R&D" cost is borne by the first to use them. Also there will be few, if any trained liquidators for the courts to hire: in Poland in mid-91 i.e. 18 months into the big bang programme there were six liquidators in the whole country.' (Rostowski, 1993, p. 9); also Abel and Gatsios (1993) on the drawbacks of bankruptcy laws too hastily designed. See also Fan and Schaffer, 1994, p. 161: 'Some of the factors behind the infrequency of bankruptcy in these countries are the practical difficulties facing creditor enterprises of pursuing debts through the courts.'

15 According to Kuznetsov (1994, p. 4), the share of defence industry employment in the overall industrial employment is about 25%.

Chapter 4: The importance of external financing

1 'This kind of import subsidisation ... did not, of course, lead directly to monetary financing, since the "enlarged deficit" was exactly matched by the foreign credit in 1992.' (Sachs, 1994b, p. 25)

2 Koen and Marrese (1995), p. 5, find different figures: 29% in 1992 from June to December, 15% in 1993 and 7% in 1994.

3 'With the change in the structure of the economy through the process of privatisation and the emergence of a large number of new, often small

enterprises, the ability of the tax administration to tax economic activity in a comprehensive way has deteriorated sharply.' (IMF, 1995, p. 13)

4 'Profit tax collections will fall because of the decree on taxation from December 1993. The decree provides numerous tax exemptions for "productive development or social construction". For example the exemptions are being given to enterprises for increasing investment and to banks which offer investment credits.' (Nagel, 1994, p. 2)

5 'Wage costs amounting to between four and eight times the minimum wage were subject to the profit tax rate of 32% and wages in excess of that were taxed at 50 percent.' (IMF, 1995, p. 15).

6 For a full discussion on the Russian excess wage tax see Shapiro and Roxburgh (1994).

7 'Agricultural subsidies remained high in 1993, although direct transfers declined, from 3.6 percent of GDP in 1992 to 2.7 percent of GDP in 1993 ... a large part of the sharp worsening in the fiscal performance was due to the granting of Rbs 1.6 trn in concessional credit from the budget to the state grain procurement agency, Rosklebprodukt, for state purchases of grain at above market prices.' (IMF, 1995, p. 18)

8 'In 1990, the Soviet government wrote off Rbs 93 bn of bad loans to the agricultural sector alone.' Hansson (1991a, p. 22), quoting the *Wall Street Journal Europe* of 6 June 1991.

9 This figure varies from source to source because Goskomstat in 1992 published four different GDP figures.

10 Amelina et al. (1993) show that the volume of grain credits from the CBR in 1992 was equivalent to about R620 billion, about half the total credits issued to the agricultural sector in 1992 and equivalent to 3.4% of GDP.

11 In order to improve the working capital position of the enterprise sector, the Economic Memorandum of June 1992 agreed with the IMF allowed for expenditures on enterprises up to a limit of R100–150 billion during the second half of 1992. At the end of August another R150 billion credit for state firms was agreed, provided that the Memorandum's global budgetary ceilings were respected.

12 Credits to the government were allocated by the CBR at an annual rate of 10% until the end of 1994. Interest on directed credits via commercial banks to enterprises was higher and varied by sector. Subsidized credits were abolished in October 1993, with the exception of credits to the government which were abolished at the beginning of 1995 in the framework of the IMF negotiations.

Chapter 5: Financial policies and exchange rate behaviour

1   'A special budgetary exchange rate of 20% of the inter bank market rate continued to apply to centralised imports until August 15 1992. The CBR also continued to calculate the official exchange rate of the former Gosbank for valuation of external claims of the former USSR.' (IMF, 1993a, p. 35) The rate of 125.26 roubles to the dollar was the 'average' in trading on MICEX.

2   During 1992 and 1993 five other exchange markets (St Petersburg, Yekaterinburg, Novosibirsk, Vladivostok and Rostov) were established. The exchange market in Vladivostok, for instance, was created in March 1993. The CBR intervenes on these markets to prevent the exchange rates deviating unduly from the Moscow rate.

3   Funds in the currency reserve were used to support the exchange rate on the internal currency market and were also for sale to the Russian Finance Ministry.

4   A comprehensive account is given in Koen and Meyermans (1994, pp. 2–4).

5   Also, 'a credit auction house specialising in small-scale transactions – the Moscow Interbank Financial House (IFH), with 80 member banks – commenced operations in November 1992, supplying bid and offer US dollar/rouble and DM/rouble rates on a daily electronic information system facilitating direct dealing among members' (Koen and Meyermans, 1994, p. 6).

6   For a full discussion, see Koen and Meyermans (1994).

7   In the last quarter of 1993, the average wage in US$ rose to $80 and $100 as the nominal exchange rate was fairly stable between R1,000 and R1,100 and the inflation rate around 20% a month.

8   IMF (1995), p. 223: 'A decree (issued on 23 May 1994) stipulated the elimination of all export quotas as of 1 July 1994. The list of strategically important goods was maintained even for goods whose exports no longer require a quota, and the licensing requirement for these goods was replaced by a registration requirement. A second decree published on 1 July 1994 postponed the elimination of export quotas on oil and oil products until 1 January 1995.'

9   See Havlik (1995), pp. 36–8 on the problems with Russian foreign trade statistics; and Kuboniwa (1995), pp. 47–50 on the reliability of foreign trade data for 1991.

10 Illarionov (1995), p. 22: 'The most drastic price reduction was for non ferrous metals, cast iron, diamonds, wood-processing products, oil and oil

products, and fertilisers.'

11 Koen and Meyermans (1994) develop an econometric model of the behaviour of the exchange rate.

12 From discussions with several Russian commercial banks, it seems that the interest rate on dollar deposits varied between 5% and 12% per year, i.e. about 0.5% per month.

13 'The expected total outstanding at the end of 1994 is around [R]11 trn or $3.5 bn i.e. 1–2% of GDP.' (Johnson and White, 1995, p. 5)

14 The annual yield is calculated as $100((100/Pb)360/n-1)$ where n is the number of days until maturity, Pb is the average price of the bond. For a discussion on the calculation of yield on government bonds in Russia, see Warner (1994), p. 13.

15 For a description of the event see Johnson and White (1995).

16 Edwards and Losada, (1994, p. 9) show that the constraint on the government is reputational.

17 On 5 July 1995 the exchange rate was restricted to fluctuations within a band – R4,300 to R4,900. This limit applied until 1 October 1995.

Chapter 6: Conclusion

1 This does not, of course, apply to people with low opportunity of time (unskilled labourers, pensioners, etc.), nor to such beneficiaries of the old system as the vast class of state administrative employees and military officers (many of whom enjoyed privileged access to goods in general shortage).

2 Hinds (1990), p. 6; Murphy et al. (1992, p. 890) showed that the incomplete price reforms in the case of the Soviet Union 'encouraged the diversion of many essential inputs away from their traditional users toward private and other enterprises who were less constrained by arbitrarily regulated prices and so could offer better deals to suppliers'.

3 The existence of a large monetary overhang is a good example of the sort of factor that sharply narrows the range of incremental options open to new reforming governments as they set about stabilization.

4 Quoted in Yeltsin (1994), p. 156; no reference is given for the source of the Gaidar article.

BIBLIOGRAPHY

Abbreviations used

CEPR	Centre for Economic Policy Research
EBRD	European Bank for Reconstruction and Development
ECARE	European Centre for Advanced Research in Economics
IIASA	International Institute for Applied Systems Analysis
IMF	International Monetary Fund
LSE	London School of Economics and Political Science
MFU	Macroeconomic and Financial Unit, Ministry of Finance of the Russian Federation
NBER	National Bureau of Economic Research
OECD	Organization for Economic Cooperation and Development
RIIA	Royal Institute of International Affairs
WIDER	World Institute for Development Economics Research

Abel, I. and Gatsios, K. (1993) 'The Economics of Bankruptcy and the Transition to a Market Economy', CEPR, London, Discussion Paper no. 878, December.

Abel, I. and Siklos, P. (1993) 'Constraints on Enterprise Liquidity and their Impact on the Monetary Reform in Formerly Centrally Planned Economies', CEPR, London, Discussion Paper no. 841, November.

Amelina, M., Galbi, D. and Uspenskii, A. (1993) 'The Distribution of Central Bank Credits for Grain Procurement', mimeo, MFU, Moscow, 3 September.

Åslund, A. (1994) 'Russia's Success Story', *Foreign Affairs*, September/October, pp. 58–71.

—(1995) *How Russia Became a Market Economy*, The Brookings Institution, Washington, DC.

Bennett, J. (1990, 'Queuing and the Price Level under Repressed Inflation', mimeo, LSE, London.

Berg, A. and Delpla, J. (1993), 'Inflation in Russia in 1992–1993: Financial

Factors in the Present Inflation', mimeo, MFU, Moscow, 28 May.

Berg, A., Delpla, J., Garbusov, Y. and Wermuth, J. (1993) 'Energy Prices and Inflation in Russia', MFU, Moscow, 26 July.

Birman, I. and Clarke, R. (1985) 'Inflation and the Money Supply in the Soviet Economy', *Soviet Studies*, vol. 37, October, pp. 494–504.

Blanchard, O. and Layard, R. (1990) 'Economic Change in Poland', LSE, London.

—(1991) 'Post-stabilisation Inflation in Poland, May 1991 - Preliminary', MIT/NBER/LSE.

Boeva, I. and Dolgopiatova, T. (1993) 'State Enterprises during Transition: Forming of Survival Strategies', paper presented at the conference on the Change of Economic System in Russia, 15–16 June, Stockholm School of Economics.

Boissieu, de C. et al. (1993) 'Inter-Enterprise Debt in Russia, 1992–1993: Presentation of Results', TACIS (EEC), Coopers & Lybrand with N.M. Rothschild, April.

Borensztein, E., Demekas, D. and Ostry, J. (1993) 'An Empirical Analysis of the Output Declines in Three Eastern European Countries', *IMF Staff Papers*, vol. 40, no. 1, March, pp. 1–31.

Boycko, M. (1991) 'Price Decontrol: The Microeconomic Case for the "Big Bang" Approach', in 'Microeconomics of Transition in Eastern Europe', *Oxford Review of Economic Policy*, vol. 7, no. 4, pp. 35–45.

—(1992) 'When Inflation Incomes Reduce Welfare: Queues, Labour Supply, and Macro-Equilibrium in Soviet-Type Economies', mimeo.

Boycko, M. and Shleifer, A. (1994) 'The Russian Restructuring and Social Assets', paper presented to the conference on Russian Economic Reforms in Jeopardy, 15–16 June, Stockholm School of Economics.

Brada, J. and King. A. (1991) 'Is There a J-Curve for the Economic Transition from Socialism to Capitalism?', World Bank, Washington, DC, Socialist Economies Reform Unit, Country Economic Department, Research Paper Series, no. 13, June.

Brainard, L.J. (1990) 'Reform in Eastern Europe: Creating a Capital Market', *Amex Bank Review*, Special Papers, no. 18, November.

Brennan, G. and Buchanan, J. (1981) 'Monopoly in Money and Inflation', *International Economic Affairs*,

Brown, A.N., Ickes, B. and Ryterman, R. (1993) 'The Myth of Monopoly: A New View of Industrial Structure in Russia', mimeo, World Bank/ University of Michigan/Pennsylvania State University, June.

Bruno, M. (1990) 'High Inflation and the Nominal Anchors of an Open

Economy', NBER, Cambridge, Working Papers no. 3518, November.

—(1992) 'Stabilization and Reform in Eastern Europe: A Preliminary Evaluation', *IMF Staff Papers*, vol. 39, no. 4, December.

Cagan, P. (1956) 'The Monetary Dynamics of Hyperinflation', in M. Friedman, ed., *Studies in the Quantity Theory of Money*, Chicago, University of Chicago Press, pp. 25–117.

Calvo, G.A. (1990) 'Are High Interest Rates Effective for Stopping High Inflation?', paper presented to seminar on Managing Inflation in Socialist Economies, Laxenburg, Austria, 6–8 March (EDI, World Bank); published in S. Commander, ed., *Managing Inflation in Socialist Economies in Transition*, Washington, DC, World Bank, 1991, pp. 247–61.

Calvo, G.A. and Coricelli, F. (1992) 'Stabilisation in Poland', *Economic Policy*, pp. 175–226, April.

—(1993) 'Output Collapse in Eastern Europe: The Role of Credit', *IMF Staff Papers*, vol. 40, no. 1, March, pp. 32–52.

Calvo, G.A. and Frenkel, J. (1991) 'From Centrally Planned to Market Economies: The Road from CPE to PCPE', *IMF Staff Papers*, June, pp. 268–99.

Calvo, G.A. and Kumar, M.S. (1994) 'Money Demand, Bank Credit and Economic Performance in Former Socialist Economies', *IMF Staff Papers*, vol. 41, no. 2, June, pp. 314–49.

Calvo, G.A. and Vegh, C. (1994) 'Inflation Stabilisation and Nominal Anchors', *Contemporary Economic Policy*, vol. 12, April, pp. 35–45.

Camen, U. and Genberg, U. (1987) 'Over- and Undervalued Currencies: Theory, Measurement, and Policy Implications', European University Institute Colloquium Papers, *IMS, EMS and Plans for World Monetary Reform*, Badia Fiesolana, 2–3 April (DOC IUE 49/87, col. 10).

Chang, G.H. (1994) 'Monetary Overhang: Do Centrally Planned Economies Have Excessive Money Stocks?', *Contemporary Economic Policy*, vol. 12, July, pp. 79–90.

Claassen, Emil M. (1992) 'Cleaning the Balance Sheets of Commercial Banks in Eastern Europe and their Role in Corporate Governance', Université de Paris-Dauphine, Paris, July.

Cochrane, J. and Ickes, B. (1991a) 'Stopping Inflation in Reforming Socialist Economies', *American Economic Review*, May.

—(1991b) 'Inflation Stabilisation in Reforming Socialist Economies: The Myth of the Monetary Overhang', *Journal of Comparative Economics*, vol. 33, pp. 97–122.

—(1994) 'Macroeconomics in Russia', mimeo, 29 July.

Collins, M. and Rodrik, D. (1991) 'Eastern Europe and the Soviet Union in the World Economy', Institute for International Economics, Washington, DC, no. 32, May.

Commander, S. and Coricelli, F. (1990a) 'The Macroeconomics of Price Reform in Socialist Countries: A Dynamic Framework', World Bank, Washington, DC, September.

—(1990b) 'Levels, Rates, and Sources of Inflation in Socialist Economies: A Dynamic Framework', paper presented to seminar on Managing Inflation in Socialist Economies, Laxenburg, Austria, 6–8 March (EDI/World Bank).

Commander, S., Liberman, L. and Yemtsov, R. (1993) 'Russia Country Study', paper prepared for workshop on Labour Markets in Transitional Socialist Economies, Stirin Castle, Czech Republic, 16–17 April (World Bank/Institute for Economic Forecasting/Russian Academy of Sciences/Moscow State University).

Commander, S. and McHale, J. (1995) 'Labor Markets in the Transition in East Europe and Russia: A Review of Experience', draft paper prepared for the World Bank *World Development Report*, 1995, Washington, DC, 3 October.

Commander, S., McHale, J. and Yemtsov, R. (1993), 'Russia', paper prepared for the World Bank conference on Unemployment, Restructuring and the Labor Market in East Europe and Russia, Washington, DC, 7–8 October.

Commander, S. and Yemtsov, R. (1992) 'Prices, Wages and Employment in Russia: Developments in 1992', World Bank/Moscow State University, Washington, DC, July.

—(1994) 'Russian Unemployment: Its Magnitude, Characteristics and Regional Dimensions', mimeo, World Bank, Washington, DC.

Commersant (1991, 1992) various issues, Moscow.

Cottarelli, C. and Blejer, M. (1992) 'Forced Saving and Repressed Inflation in the Soviet Union, 1986–90', *IMF Staff Papers*, vol. 39, no. 2, pp. 256–86, June.

Deaton, A. and Muellbauer, J., eds (1980), *Economics and Consumer Behaviour*, Cambridge, Cambridge University Press; repr. 1989.

Delovoi Mir (1992, 1993) various issues, Moscow.

Delpla, J. (1993) 'Price Policy', mimeo, MFU, Moscow.

Dewatripont, M. and Roland, G. (1993) 'The Design of Reform Packages under Uncertainty', mimeo, ECARE, Brussels, March.

Dinopoulos, E. and Lane, T. (1992) 'Market Liberalisation Policies in a Reforming Socialist Economy', *IMF Staff Papers*, vol. 39, no. 3, September.

Dornbusch, R. (1976) 'Expectations and Exchange Rate Dynamics', *Journal of Political Economy*, vol. 84, pp. 1161–76.

—(1983) 'Flexible Exchange Rates and Interdependence', *IMF Staff Papers*, vol. 30, pp. 3–30.

—(1985) 'Stopping Hyperinflation: Lessons from the German Inflation Experience of the 1920s', NBER, Cambridge, MA, Working Paper no. 1675.

—(1990a) 'Economic Reform in Eastern Europe and the Soviet Union: Priorities and Strategy', paper presented to the conference on The Transition to a Market Economy in Eastern and Central Europe, Paris, November (OECD).

—(1990b) 'Experiences with Extreme Monetary Instability', CEPR, London, Discussion Paper no. 455, September.

—(1990c) 'Credibility and Stabilisation', CEPR, London, Discussion Paper no. 343, September.

—(1992a) 'Monetary Problems of Post-Communism: Lessons from the End of the Austro-Hungarian Empire', *Weltwirtschaftliches Archiv*, vol. 128, no. 3, pp. 391–424.

—(1992b) 'A Payments Mechanism for the Commonwealth and Eastern Europe', mimeo, MIT, January.

—(1992c) 'Lessons from Experiences with High Inflation', *World Bank Review*, vol. 6, no. 1, pp. 13–31.

Dornbusch, R., Sturzenegger, F. and Wolf, H. (1990) 'Extreme Inflation: Dynamics and Stabilisation', *Brookings Papers on Economic Activity*, vol. 2, pp. 1–84.

Drebentsov, V. (1995) 'Russia's Commercial Policy from 1992 to 1994', in Janos Gacs and M.J. Peck eds, *International Trade Issues of the Russian Federation*, CP-95-2, March, International Institute for Applied Systems Analysis (IIASA), Laxenburg, Austria, pp. 173–96.

Duchene, A and Senik-Leygonie, C. (1991), 'Price Liberalization and Redeployment in the USSR, the Soviet Economy at World Prices', mimeo, EEC, Brussels, May.

Easterly, W. and Vieira da Cunha, P. (1993), 'Financing the Storm: Macroeconomic Crisis in Russia, 1992–1993', mimeo, World Bank, Washington, DC.

Economic Commission for Europe (ECE) (1992) 'Macroeconomic

Stabilization: Efforts and Results', *Economic Bulletin for Europe*, United Nations, Geneva, pp. 91–101.

Edwards, S. and Losada, F. (1994) 'Fixed Exchange Rates, Inflation and Macroeconomic Discipline', NBER, Cambridge, MA, Working Paper no. 4661, February.

Ellam, M. and Layard, R. (1992) 'Prices, Incomes and Hardship', MS, Stockholm Institute of East European Economies.

Ericson, R.E. (1991) 'The Classical Soviet-Type Economy: Nature of the System and Implications for Reform', draft, 15 February.

European Economy (1990), 'Stabilization, Liberalization and Devolution: Assessment of the Economic Situation and Reform Process in the Soviet Union', no. 45, December.

Fan, Q. and Schaffer, M. (1994) 'Government Financial Transfers and Enterprise Adjustements in Russia, with Comparisons to Central and Eastern Europe', *Economies of Transition*, vol. 2, no. 2, pp. 151–88.

Fender, J. and Laing, D. (1992) 'The Macroeconomics of a Reforming Centrally Planned Economy with Queuing and Resale', Pennsylvania State University, Working Paper, April.

Fishlow, A. and Friedman, J. (1994) 'Tax Evasion, Inflation and Stabilisation', *Journal of Development Economics*, vol. 43, pp. 105–23.

Freinkman, L. (1994) 'Government Financial Transfers to the Enterprise Sector', in 'Russia: General Trends and Influence on Country Macroeconomic Performance', mimeo, World Bank, Washington, DC, May.

Fry, M.J. (1993) 'The Fiscal Abuse of Central Banks', IMF Working Paper no. 58, IMF, Washington, DC, July.

Fry, M.J. and Nuti, M.D. (1992) 'Monetary and Exchange Rate Policies during Eastern Europe's Transition: Some Lessons from Further East', *Oxford Review of Economic Policy*, vol. 8, no. 1, pp. 27–43.

Fyodorov, B. (1994) 'Macroeconomic Policy and Stabilisation in Russia', paper presented to the conference on Russian Economic Reforms in Jeopardy, 15–16 June, Stockholm School of Economics, Stockholm.

Gavrilenkov, E. and Koen, V. (1994) 'How Large was the Output Collapse in Russia? Alternative Estimates and Welfare Implications', mimeo, IMF, Washington, DC, 17 November.

Genberg, H. (1991), 'On the Sequencing of Reforms in Eastern Europe', IMF Working Papers, no. 13, IMF, Washington, DC.

Gold, J. (1971) *The Fund's Concept of Convertibility*, Pamphlet Series no. 14, IMF, Washington, DC.

—(1981) *Finance and Development*, September.

Goldberg, L. (1992) 'Moscow Black Markets and Official Markets for Foreign Exchange: How Much Flexibility in Flexible Rates?' NBER, Cambridge, MA, Working Paper no. 4040, March.

Goldberg, L. and Karimov, I. (1992) 'Black Markets for Currency, Hoarding Activity and Policy Reforms', IIASA, Laxenburg, Austria, Working Paper no. 92–044, July.

Goldberg L. and Tenorio R. (1995) 'Explaining Order Imbalances in Russia's Tâtonnement Foreign Exchange Auction', in Janos Gacs and M.J. Peck, eds, *International Trade Issues of the Russian Federation*, CP-95-2, March, International Institute for Applied Systems Analysis (IIASA), Laxenburg, Austria, pp. 138–59.

Goskomstat RF (1991–4) *Russian Statistical Yearbook* for 1990, 1991, 1992, 1993, 1994, Moscow.

Granville, B. (1990) 'Convertibility and Exchange Rates in Poland: 1957–1990', RIIA, London, Discussion Paper no. 33.

—(1992) 'Price and Currency Reform in the CIS', RIIA, London, Post-Soviet Business Forum paper.

—(1993) 'Russian Monetary Policy in 1992: The Threat to Stabilisation', *Business Strategy Review*, London Business School.

—(1994) 'So Farewell Rouble Zone', paper prepared for the conference on Russian Economic Reforms in Jeopardy, 15–16 June, Stockholm School of Economics, Stockholm.

Granville, B. and Lushin, A. (1993), 'The New Style Rouble Zone or the Old Soviet Union "Revisited" ', mimeo, MFU, Moscow, 15 October.

Granville, B. and Shapiro, J. (1994) 'Russian Inflation: A Statistical Pandora's Box', RIIA, London, Discussion Paper no. 53.

Greene, J.E. and Isard, P. (1991) 'Currency Convertibility and the Transformation of Centrally Planned Economies', IMF Occasional Paper no. 81, June.

Gros, D. and Steinherr, A. (1991a) 'Economic Reform in the Soviet Union: Pas de Deux between Disintegration and Macroeconomic Destabilization', *Princeton Studies in International Finance*, no. 71, November.

—(1991b) *From Centrally Planned to Market Economies: Issues for the Transition in Central Europe and the Soviet Union*, CEPS paper, London, Brasseys.

Guzhvin, P. (1992) 'Trust in Statistics', Goskomstat of the Russian Federation, *Statistical Bulletin*, no. 9, pp. 3–21 (in Russian).

Hansson, A. (1991a) 'Monetary Reform in a Newly Independent State: The Case of Estonia', mimeo, WIDER, 15 October.

—(1991b) 'The Emergence and Stabilisation of Extreme Inflationary Pressures in the Soviet Union', United Nations University, Helsinki, WIDER Working Papers no. 93, September.

—(1992) 'The Trouble with the Rouble: Monetary Reform in the Former Soviet Union', Stockholm Institute of Soviet and East European Economics, Working Paper no. 57; paper originally presented to the conference on the Change of Economic System in Russia, 15–16 June, Stockholm School of Economics.

Hansson, A. and Sachs, J. (1992) 'The Case of National Currencies in the Former Soviet Union: Crowning the Estonian Kroon', *Transition*, vol. 3, no. 9, October.

—(1994) 'Monetary Institutions and Credible Stabilisation: A Comparison of Experiences in the Baltics', June; revised version of paper presented at conference on Central Banks in Eastern Europe and the Newly Independent States, University of Chicago Law School, 22–3 April.

Hardy, D. (1992) 'Soft Budget Constraints, Firm Commitments, and the Social Safety Net', *IMF Staff Papers*, vol. 39, no. 2, June, pp. 310–29.

Hardy, D. and Lahiri, K. (1992) 'Bank Insolvency and Stabilisation in Eastern Europe', *IMF Staff Papers*, vol. 39, no. 4, December, pp. 778–800.

Havlik, P. (1995) 'Russian Foreign Trade Reflected in Statistics', in Janos Gacs and M.J. Peck, eds, *International Trade Issues of the Russian Federation*, CP-95-2, March, International Institute for Applied Systems Analysis (IIASA), Laxenburg, Austria, pp. 28–42.

Hinds, M. (1990) *Issues in the Introduction of Market Forces in Eastern European Socialist Economies*, EMTTF, World Bank Report, January.

Ickes, B.W. and Ryterman, R. (1992) *Inter-Enterprise Arrears and Financial Underdevelopment in Russia*, IMF Research Department, Washington, DC, 16 September.

Illarionov, A. (1995) 'Foreign Trade in Russia: 1992–1993', in Janos Gacs and M.J. Peck, eds, *International Trade Issues of the Russian Federation*, CP-95-2, March, International Institute for Applied Systems Analysis (IIASA), Laxenburg, Austria, pp. 9–27.

IMF (1988) *Yearbook of Foreign Exchange Restrictions*, IMF, Washington, DC.

—(1992a) *Economic Review: Russian Federation*, April.

—(1992b) 'Money and Banking Statistics in Former Soviet Union (FSU) Economies', prepared by R. Calogero, W. Nahr and T.R. Stillson, authorized for distribution by J.B. McLenaghan, WP/02/103, December.

—(1993a) *Russian Federation*, IMF Economic Reviews, no. 8, June.

—(1993b) *IMF World Outlook*, May.

—(1994) *Financial Relations among Countries of the Former Soviet Union*, IMF Economic Reviews, no. 1, February.

—(1995) *Russian Federation*, IMF Economic Reviews, no. 16, March.

IMF, World Bank, OECD and EBRD (1990) *The Economy of the USSR: Summary and Recommendations*, World Bank, Washington, DC.

Interfax (1991–3) various issues, Moscow.

Izvestia (1991, 1992, 1993) various issues, Moscow.

Johnson, H.G. (1965) 'Is Inflation the Inevitable Price of Rapid Development or a Retarding Factor in Economic Growth?', in *Essays in Monetary Economics*, London, Allen, ch. 9, pp. 281–91.

—(1968) 'Problems of Efficiency in Monetary Management', *Journal of Political Economy*, vol. 76, September/October, pp. 971–90.

Johnson, S. and White, G. (1995) 'Emerging Financial Markets in Russia', mimeo, Institute of Economic Analysis, Moscow/Fuqua School of Business, Duke University.

Keynes, J.M. (1923) *A Tract on Moneetary Reform*, repr. London, Royal Economic Society, 1974.

—(1925) *A Short View on Russia*, London, Leonard and Virginia Woolf.

Khoo, L. and Tsepliaeva, J. (1994) 'An Explanation for the High Levels of Excess Reserves in Post-Transition Russia: 1992 to 1994', mimeo, Harvard University/New Economic School, Moscow.

Koen, V. (1994) 'Measuring the Transition: A User's View on National Accounts in Russia', IMF Working Paper no. 6, January.

Koen, V. and Marrese, M. (1995) 'Stabilisation and Structural Change in Russia, 1992–1994', IMF Working Paper no. 13, January.

Koen, V. and Meyermans, E. (1994) 'Exchange Rate Determinants In Russia: 1992–1993', IMF Working Paper no. 66, June.

Koen, V. and Phillips, S. (1993) *Price Liberalisation in Russia: Behavior of Prices, Household Incomes and Consumption during the First Year*, IMF Occasional Paper no. 104, June.

Kornai, J. (1980) *Economics of Shortage*, Amsterdam/New York, North-Holland.

—(1982) *Growth, Shortage and Efficiency: A Macrodynamic Model of the Socialist Economy*, Oxford, Oxford University Press.

—(1986) 'The Soft Budget Constraint', *Kyklos*, vol. 39, no. 1, pp. 3–30.

Kuboniwa, M. (1995) 'The Structure of Foreign Trade Statistics', in Janos Gacs and M.J. Peck, eds, *International Trade Issues of the Russian Federation*, CP-95-2, March, International Institute for Applied Systems Analysis (IIASA), Laxenburg, Austria, pp. 43-68.

Kuznetsov, Y. (1994) 'Adjustment of the Russian Defence-Related Enterprises in 1992–1993: Macroeconomic Implications', paper prepared for the conference on Restructuring and Recovery of Output in Russia, 9–11 June (IIASA).

Lane, T. (1992) 'Household Demand for Money in Poland: Theory and Evidence', *IMF Staff Papers*, vol. 39, no. 4, December, pp. 825–54.

Lange, O. (1937) 'On the Economic Theory of Socialism', *Review of Economic Studies*, vol. 4, no. 1, October.

Lanyi, A. (1969) 'The Case for Floating Exchange Rates Reconsidered', *Essays*, Princeton University, International Finance Section, no. 72, February.

Layard, R. (1993) 'Can Russia Control Inflation?', paper presented to the conference on A Framework for Monetary Stability, October (The Netherlands Bank).

Layard, R. and Richter, A. (1994) 'Labour Market Adjustment: The Russian Way', paper presented at the conference on Russian Reforms in Jeopardy, 15–16 June, Stockholm School of Economics.

Lequiller, F. and Zieschang, K. D. (1994), 'Drift in Producer Price Indexes for the Former Soviet Union (FSU) Countries', IMF Working Papers, no. 35, March.

Lin, S. (1993) 'A Monetary Model of a Shortage Economy', *IMF Staff Papers*, vol. 40, no. 2, June, pp. 369–94.

Linz, S. (1990) 'The Soviet Economy in Transition: A Resurgence of Reform', Michigan State University, Econometrics and Economic Theory Paper no. 8901.

Lipton, D. and Sachs, J. (1990) *Creating a Market Economy in Eastern Europe: The Case of Poland*, Brookings Papers on Economic Activity, no. 1, Washington, DC.

—(1992) 'Prospects for Russia's Economic Reforms', mimeo prepared for the Brookings Panel on Economic Activity, 17–18 September, Washington, DC.

McKinnon, R. (1991) 'Stabilising the Ruble: The Problem of Internal Currency Convertibility', in E.M. Claassen, ed., *Exchange Rate Policies in Developing and Post-Socialist Countries*, International Centre for Economic Growth/ICS Press, San Francisco, CA, pp. 59–87.

—(1993), 'Gradual versus Rapid Liberalization in Socialist Economies: Financial Policies and Macroeconomic Stability in China and Russia Compared', paper prepared for presentation at World Bank Annual Conference on Development Economics, 3–4 May, Washington, DC; revised 18 May.

Melitz, J. and Waysand, C. (1994) 'The Role of Government Aid to Firms during the Transition to a Market Economy: Russia 1992–1994', CREST/INSEE, Paris, Working Document no. 9435.

Michalopoulos, C. and Tarr, D. (1992) 'Transitional Trade and Payments Arrangements for States of the Former USSR', mimeo, World Bank, Washington, DC, June.

Milesi-Feretti, G. M. (1992), 'Wage Claims, Incomes Policy and the Path of Output and Inflation in a Formerly Centrally Planned Economy', Centre for Economic Performance, LSE, Discussion Paper no. 106, November.

Mises, L. von (1920) 'Economic Calculation in the Socialist Commonwealth', in F.A. von Hayek, ed., *Collectivist Economic Planning*, London, Routledge & Kegan Paul, 1935, pp. 89–130; quoted here from A. Nove and D.M. Nuti, eds, *Socialist Economics: Selected Readings*, Harmondsworth, Penguin, 1972, pp. 75–81; first publ. in German in *Archiv für Sozialwissenschaften*.

Mourmouras, A. and Tijerina, J. (1994) 'Collection Lags and the Optimal Inflation Tax: A Reconsideration', *IMF Staff Papers*, vol. 41, no. 1, March.

Murphy, K., Shleifer, A. and Vishny, R. (1992) 'The Transition to a Market Economy: Pitfalls of Partial Reform', *Quarterly Journal of Economcis*, vol. 107, no. 3, August, pp. 889–906.

Murrell, P. (1990), *Big Bang versus Evolution: Eastern European Reforms in the Light of Recent Economic History*, PlanEcon Report, Washington, DC, 29 June.

Nagel, M. (1994), 'Budget Revenue, 1993–1994', unpublished mimeo, Moscow, 19 March.

Nagel, M., Dvorkovich, A., Fominikh, K., Hedback, T. and Neuber, A. (1993) 'Basic Principles of Fiscal Federalism', mimeo, MFU, Moscow, 12 August.

NATO Economic Committee (1992) *Soviet Economic Performance in 1991: A Weak Foundation for a New Political Beginning*, Brussels, NATO, January.

Nuti, D.M. (1986) 'Hidden and Repressed Inflation in Soviet-Type Economies: Definitions, Measurements and Stabilisation', *Contributions to Political Economy*, vol. 5, March, pp. 37–82.

—(1990a) 'Internal and International Aspects of Monetary Disequilibrium in Poland', in Commission of the European Communities, *Economic Transformation in Hungary and Poland: European Economy*, no. 43, March, pp. 181–96.

—(1990b) 'Stabilisation and Sequencing in the Reform of Socialist

Economies', paper presented to seminar on Managing Inflation in Socialist Economies, Laxenburg, Austria, 6–8 March (EDI/World Bank).

—(1991) 'Privatisation of Socialist Economies: General Issues and the Polish Case', in H. Blommestein and M. Marrese, eds, *Transformation of Planned Economies: Property Rights Reform and Macroeconomic Stability*, Paris, OECD.

Oblath, G. (1988) 'Exchange Rate Policy in the Reform Package', *Acta Oeconomica*, vol. 39, nos 1–2, pp. 81–93.

OECD (1989) 'East–West Trade and Financial Relations Developments in 1987–88 and Future Prospects', *Financial Market Trends*, February.

—(1992a) *Short Term Economic Statistics, Central and Eastern Europe*, Paris.

—(1992b) *Short Term Economic Indicators, Central and Eastern Europe*, Paris.

Ofer, G. (1992) 'Macroeconomic Stabilisation and Structural Change: Orthodox, Heterodox or Otherwise?', paper presented at the Tenth World Congress of the International Economic Association, Moscow, 24–28 August.

Oppenheimer, P. (1992) 'Economic Reform in Russia', *National Institute Economic Review*, August, pp. 48–61.

Ortuno-Ortin, I., Roemer, J.E. and Silvestre, J. (1990) 'Market Socialism', University of California, Berkeley, Department of Economics, Working Paper no. 356, 27 March.

Osband, K. (1992a) 'Economic Crisis in a Shortage Economy', *Journal of Political Economy*, vol. 100, no. 4, pp. 673–90.

—(1992b) 'Index Number Biases during Price Liberalisation', *IMF Staff Papers*, vol. 39, no. 2, June, pp. 287–309.

Popov, V. (1994) 'Central Bank Independence and Inflation in Russia', paper presented at conference on Central Banks in Eastern Europe and the NIS, Chicago, 21–23 April.

Portes, R. (1974) 'Macroeconomic Equilibrium under Central Planning', Institute for International Studies, University of Stockholm, Seminar Paper no. 40.

—(1989) 'The Theory and Measurement of Macroeconomic Disequilibrium in Centrally Planned Economies', in Christopher Davis and Wojciech Charemza, eds, *Models of Disequilibrium and Shortage in Centrally Planned Economies*, London/New York, Chapman & Hall.

—(1991) 'The Path to Reform in Central and Eastern Europe: An Introduction', CEPR, London, Discussion Paper no. 559.

Richter, R. (1991) 'A Socialist Market Economy: Can It Work?', Hoover Institution, Stanford University, Working Papers in Economics E-91-4, February.

Robinson, D.J. and Stella, P. (1988) 'Amalgamating Central Bank and Fiscal Deficits', in Mario I. Blejer and Ke-Young Chu, eds, *Measurement of Fiscal Impact: Methodological Issues*, Washington, DC, IMF, June, pp. 20–31.

Rodrik, D. (1992a) 'Foreign Trade in Eastern Europe's Transition: Early Results', paper presented to conference on Transition in Eastern Europe, 26–29 February (NBER).

—(1992b) 'Making Sense of the Soviet Trade Shock in Eastern Europe: A Framework and Some Estimates', paper prepared for the World Bank/ IMF conference on The Macroeconomic Situation in Eastern Europe, Washington, DC, May.

Roland, G. (1990) 'Report to the EEC on the Political Economy of the Transition Period in the Soviet Union', mimeo, November.

Rollo, J.M.C. (1992) *Association Agreements between the EC and the CSFR, Hungary and Poland: A Half Empty Glass?*, London, RIIA.

Rosefielde, S. and Pfouts, W. (1989) 'Rouble Convertibility: Demand Responsive Exchange Rates in a Goal-Directed Economy', *European Economic Review*, vol. 34 [1990], pp. 1377–97.

Rostowski, J. (1993) 'The Inter-Enterprise Debt Explosion in the Former Soviet Union: Causes, Consequences, Cures', mimeo, IMF, Washington, DC.

Russian Economic Trends (1992, vol. 1, nos 1–4; 1993, vol. 2, nos 1–4; 1994, vol. 3, nos 1–4) produced by the Centre for Economic Performance, LSE, London and the Russian government's Working Centre for Economic Reform, Moscow.

Sachs, J. (1993) 'Achieving Monetary Stabilization in Russia in 1993', mimeo, Harvard University.

—(1994a) Testimony to the Banking Committee, US Senate, 5 February, Harvard University.

—(1994b) 'Russia's Struggle with Stabilisation: Conceptual Issues and Evidence', paper prepared for the World Bank's Annual Conference on Development Economics, 28–29 April, Washington, DC.

—(1994c) 'Towards Glasnost in the IMF', *Challenge*, May–June, pp. 4–11.

Sachs, J. and Lipton, D. (1992) 'Remaining Steps to a Market-Based Monetary System in Russia', Working Paper no. 54, Stockholm Institute of East European Economics; paper also presented at the conference on The Change of Economic System in Russia, 15–16 June, Stockholm School of Economics.

Sapir, J. (1992) 'Inflation, Depression and Stabilization in Russia: Why Traditional Macroeconomics Have Failed', paper presented to the

French-CIS seminar on Monetary and Financial Issues under the Transition, 7–9 December, Moscow.

Sarafanov, M. (1995) 'Russia's Actual and Potential Role in International Capital Flows', in Janos Gacs and M.J. Peck, eds, *International Trade Issues of the Russian Federation*, CP-95-2, March, International Institute for Applied Systems Analysis (IIASA), Laxenburg, Austria, pp. 239–49.

Sargent, T. (1982), 'The Ends of Four Big Inflations', in R.E. Hall, ed., *Inflation: Causes and Effects*, Chicago, Chicago University Press.

Sargent, T. and Wallace, N. (1981) 'Some Unpleasant Monetarist Arithmetic', *FRBM Quarterly Review*, pp. 1–17.

Shapiro, J. and Roxburgh, I. (1994) 'Employment Incentives of the Russian Excess Wages Tax', mimeo, MFU, Moscow/University of London.

Schneider, C. (1994) 'Western Assistance to Central and Eastern European Countries in their Transition to Market Systems', IIASA, Laxenburg, Austria, Working Paper no. 94–006, February.

Schrettle, W. (1990) 'Transition in Depression: Soviet Monetary Issues', Osteuropea Institut München, Working Paper no. 40, October.

Shleifer, A. and Vishny, R. (1991) 'Reversing the Current Soviet Economic Collapse', *Brookings Papers on Economic Activity*, no. 2, pp. 341–60.

Smith, A. (1993) *Russia and the World Economy: Problems of Integration*, London/New York, Routledge.

Sutela P. (1995) 'Policy Making and the Evolution of Foreign Trade Regimes', in Janos Gacs and M.J. Peck, eds, *International Trade Issues of the Russian Federation*, CP-95-2, March, International Institute for Applied Systems Analysis (IIASA), Laxenburg, Austria, pp. 89–110.

Tait, A.A. (1993) 'Enterprise Behavior under Conditions of Economic Growth in the Russian Federation: Taxation', IMF, August, paper prepared for the workshop on Enterprise Behavior under the Conditions of Economic Reform in the Russian Federation, Laxenburg, Austria, 6–8 July (IIASA).

Tanzi, V. (1978) 'Inflation, Real Tax Revenue and the Case for Inflationary Finance: Theory with an Application to Argentina', *IMF Staff Papers*, vol. 25, September, pp. 417–51.

—(1991) 'Tax Reform in Economies in Transition: A Brief Introduction to the Main Issues', IMF Working Paper no. 23, March.

—(1993) 'The Budget Deficit in Transition: A Cautionary Note', *IMF Staff Papers*, vol. 40, no. 3, September, pp. 697–707.

Tanzi, V., Blejer, M. and Teijero, M. (1988), 'The Effects of Inflation on the Measurement of Fiscal Deficits', in Mario I. Blejer and Ke-young Chu, eds, *Measurement of Fiscal Impact: Methodological Issues*, Washington, DC, IMF, June.

Tobin, J. (1969) 'A General Equilibrium Approach to Monetary Theory', *Journal of Money, Credit and Banking*, vol. 1, February.

Transition (1990, 1991, 1992) Washington, DC, World Bank.

Trzeciakowski, W. (1965) 'The Model of Current Optimum Version in Foreign Trade and its Application', *American Review of Soviet and East European Foreign Trade*, vol. 1, no. 2, pp. 42–66 (trans. from Russian).

—(1978) *Indirect Management in a Centrally Planned Economy*, Amsterdam, North-Holland.

Vavilov, A. and Vjugin, O. (1991) 'Inflation in the USSR', mimeo, study for the EC Commission, Moscow, October.

Vegh, C. (1992) 'Stopping High Inflation: An Analytical Overview', *IMF Staff Papers*, vol. 39, no. 3, September, pp. 626–95.

Warner, A. (1994), 'The Russian Partial Stabilisation', mimeo, Institute for Economic Analysis, Moscow/Harvard University.

Wattleworth, M. (1988), 'Credit Subsidies in Budgetary Lending: Computation, Effects and Fiscal Implications', in Mario I. Blejer and Ke-Young Che, eds, *Measurement of Fiscal Impact: Methodological Issues*, Washington, DC, IMF, June, pp. 57–70.

Weitzman, M. (1990) 'Price Distortion and Shortage Deformation or What Happened to the Soap?', Harvard University, Harvard Institute of Economic Research, Discussion Paper no. 1472, March.

Wijnbergen, S. van (1991) 'Fiscal Deficits, Exchange Rate Crises and Inflation', *Review of Economic Studies*, vol. 58, pp. 81–92.

Williamson, J. (1991) 'Advice on the Choice of an Exchange Rate Policy', in E.M. Claassen, ed., *Exchange Rate Policies in Developing and Post-Socialist Countries*, San Francisco, International Center for Economic Growth.

—(1992a) BP lecture, LSE, 24–5 February.

—(1992b) 'Why Did Output Fall in Eastern Europe?', paper prepared for the Arne Ryde Symposium on The Transition Problem, Rungsted Kyst, Denmark, 11–12 June.

Wolf, T.A. (1985a) 'Economic Stabilisation in Planned Economies: Toward an Analytical Framework', *IMF Staff Papers*, vol. 32, no. 1, pp. 78–131.

—(1985b) 'Exchange Rate Systems and Adjustment in Planned Economies', *IMF Staff Papers*, vol. 32, no. 2, pp. 211–47.

—(1990) 'The Exchange Rate and the Price Level in Socialist Economies', paper presented to seminar on Managing Inflation in Socialist Economies, Laxenburg, Austria, 6–8 March (EDI/World Bank).

World Bank (1991) *The Transformation of Economies in Eastern and Central Europe: Issues, Progress and Prospects*, Washington, DC, April.

—(1992) *Russian Economic Reform: Crossing the Threshold of Structural Change*, a World Bank Country Study, Washington, DC, September.

World Bank and IMF (1993) 'Subsidies and Directed Credits to Enterprises in Russia: A Strategy for Reform', Washington, DC, March.

Yeltsin, B. (1994), *The View from the Kremlin*, London, HarperCollins.

Yemtsov, R. (1994) 'Ingoing and Outgoing Flows in Employment', paper prepared for the workshop on Restructuring and Recovering of Output in Russia, Laxenburg, Austria, 9–11 June (IIASA).

Zhukov, S. (1993), 'Monetary Aspects of Russian Transition', United Nations University, Helsinki, WIDER Working Paper no. 106, June.

RIIA Discussion Paper

THE ROYAL INSTITUTE OF INTERNATIONAL AFFAIRS

also by Brigitte Granville ...

Brigitte Granville and Judith Shapiro

RUSSIAN INFLATION
A Statistical Pandora's Box

CONTENTS

The inflation rate has been the most significant economic indicator in post-communist Russia. This paper analyses the course of the very high inflation in 1992 and 1993, focusing on the problematic nature of current Russian price statistics.

The paper argues that the main cause of this inflation is to be found in the increase of the money supply generated by large credits to state industry and to agriculture. These credits were supposed to avoid a collapse of production, and thus to avert unemployment. In fact, the credits primarily maintained real balances of these sectors, with the obvious result of continued inflation, leading to calls for more credits to restore the value of real balances.

The paper contends that since Russian foreign policy has focused so sharply on the issue of control of inflation, it is crucial that the measure of price movements should be appropriate to the intense use made of it. The primary purpose of the study is, therefore, to begin to understand how the Russian price index is calculated, and to raise some questions about its accuracy.

Discussion Paper No. 53
36 pages

November 1994   RIIA   Price £6.00

RIIA Special
Paper

 THE ROYAL INSTITUTE OF
INTERNATIONAL AFFAIRS

ILLUSIONS OF LIBERALIZATION
Securities Regulation in Japan and the EC

Benn Steil

AS FEATURED IN *THE FINANCIAL TIMES*, 16 MAY 1995

'Benn Steil's well-written and well-documented paper provides a useful corrective to the widely held notion that financial markets in the leading OECD countries are now substantially free. He shows that both in Japan and in the EC's Single Market strong elements of regulation remain which serve to limit competition and innovation. In both cases reforms still have a long way to go, and to have brought this out is a real contribution to better understanding of the issues' – **Professor David Henderson**, *former Chief Economist, OECD*

Rapidly rising share prices in the 1980s served to hide significant inefficiencies in the Japanese securities markets, many of which derive directly from the operation of the regulatory system. While these inefficiencies are becoming increasingly costly and transparent in the more sober market environment of the 1990s, the regulatory structure at the heart of the problem remains fundamentally untouched. The European Community, meanwhile, is working to construct a Community-wide regulatory umbrella for securities markets, and is in danger of succumbing to the most damaging tendency of the Japanese authorities. This is to view the markets not in terms of their ultimate sevices, but rather in terms of the interests of incumbent service providers. Directives which are supposed to facilitate free and open cross-border competition are instead being used to protect Member State producer interests.

This paper – the fourth to be produced by the RIIA in conjunction with the Japan Institute of International Affairs – critically examines the regulatory reform process in the Japanese and EC securities sectors. Market participants, regulators, policy-makers and researchers will find it an invaluable piece of economic and political analysis.

ISBN 0 905031 96 2 (pbk); 56 pages

April 1995   RIIA   Price £9.50

Chatham House Paper · THE ROYAL INSTITUTE OF INTERNATIONAL AFFAIRS

from the Chatham House Papers series ...

RUSSIANS BEYOND RUSSIA

Neil Melvin

The Politics of National Identity

Many ethnic Russians have, since 1992, found themselves living in non-Russian nation-states. This book analyses the political issues that surround their position, and focuses on three areas: relations between expatriate Russian-speaking communities and their host populations; the impact of expatriate issues on Russian domestic politics, such as the sensitive issue of Crimea; and the role of the new Russian diaspora in relations between the states of the former Soviet Union. Detailed case-studies explore the development of a national identity within the Russian-speaking communities of five former Soviet republics: Estonia, Kazakhstan, Latvia, Moldova and Ukraine.

Neil Melvin currently holds a British Academy Research Fellowship in the Department of Government at the London School of Economics. He has also been a Visiting Fellow at the Russian Research Center, Harvard University, and a Research Fellow at the Royal Institute of International Affairs.

ISBN 1 85567 233 2 (pbk); 144 pages

September 1995   RIIA/Pinter   Price £9.99